Your Malvern (
for GCSE

CW01663328

Spanish Speaking Test

John Connor
in association with
Val Levick
Glenise Radford
Alasdair McKeane

MALVERN LANGUAGE GUIDES
MLG

Introduction

This is a book which aims to help you with your GCSE Spanish Speaking Test. The test will probably be conducted by your own teacher and will be tape-recorded. You will have to complete a number of role-plays and a conversation test. Candidates are also required to give a presentation on a chosen topic and then discuss it. Check the exact details of your specification with your teacher. Knowing what to expect is half the battle.

This book is in four sections.

In the **Role-Play** section you will find the Spanish phrases you may need to use or understand in each situation. They are given in the *tú* and *usted (Vd.)* form where appropriate.

In the **General Conversation** section you will find straightforward questions and possible answers for most topics, again with *tú* and *usted (Vd.)* forms where appropriate. Check with your teacher which he/she is most likely to use in the Speaking Test. There are also more open-ended questions together with suitable answers, and questions where you are asked to give and justify your opinion.

The **Presentations** section has some suggestions for topics which you may wish to prepare. The usual format for the exams which include this test is that you talk for a minute or a minute and a half introducing the theme, and then discuss it with your teacher for another couple of minutes. It is also possible to use some of the topics from the Conversation section for this exercise.

The **Improving your language** section is aimed at making what you say more interesting. Phrases which extend the variety and range of structures and vocabulary in your Spanish are included. This section will be of most use to Higher Level candidates.

This book is intended to help you do well. Merely owning it will not help you! Reading, learning and practising its contents will.

¡Buena suerte!

SECTION 1: ROLE PLAY

All-purpose phrases

These phrases or part-phrases are essential. They could appear in many of the role play situations. Remember to learn how to ask questions as well as answer them.

Social remarks

Good morning .... Buenos días
Good afternoon .... Buenas tardes
Good evening .... Buenas tardes
Hello............................. ¡Hola!
How are you? .... ¿Qué tal?
Please .... Por favor
Thank you .... Gracias
Not at all....................... De nada
You are very kind......... Eres/Es muy amable
Excuse me .... Perdóna(me)
I would like … .... Quisiera …
May I …? .... ¿Puedo …?
Please come in .... Pase, por favor
Sit down .... Siéntate/Siéntese
I'm sorry, but … .... Lo siento, pero …
Don't mention it! .... De nada
Good-bye...................... Adiós
See you soon .... ¡Hasta pronto!
See you tomorrow .... ¡Hasta mañana!

Best Wishes

Good Luck! .... ¡Buena suerte!
Happy Birthday!........... ¡Feliz cumpleaños!
Happy Christmas! .... ¡Feliz Navidad!
Happy New Year! .... ¡Feliz Año Nuevo!
Have a nice day!.......... ¡Que tengas/tenga un buen día!

Questions

Why?............................ ¿Por qué?
When?.......................... ¿Cuándo?
Where?......................... ¿Dónde?
What?........................... ¿Qué?
What?........................... ¿Cómo?
Who?............................ ¿Quién? ¿Quiénes?
How much/How many? ¿Cuánto/a/os/as?
How?............................ ¿Cómo?
What is … like? .... ¿Cómo es …?
Is there/Are there …?... ¿Hay …?

Agreeing and sympathising

Yes, of course.............. Claro
Agreed.......................... De acuerdo
What a shame!............. ¡Qué lástima!
It doesn't matter .... No importa
I don't mind.................. Me da igual
I suppose so.................. Supongo que sí
I suppose so.................. Creo que sí
With pleasure .... Con mucho gusto
Yes, I'd like to............. Sí, me gustaría mucho
Good idea!..................... ¡Buena idea!
Too bad .... ¡Qué pena!
Really? .... ¿De veras?
That's nice! .... ¡Qué bien!
OK................................. Vale
Agreed.......................... Conforme
Congratulations!........... ¡Felicidades!

Apologising

I'm sorry....................... Lo siento
I'm sorry....................... ¡Perdón!
No harm done.............. No pasa nada
It doesn't matter .... No importa
Don't mention it........... No importa
Don't worry.................. No te preocupes
Let's forget it................ ¡Pelillos a la mar!
I'm sorry, but it can't be helped .... Te pido perdón, pero no hay más remedio
I didn't do it on purpose.................. No lo hice a propósito

Opinions

What is your opinion?.. ¿Qué opinas?
I like .... Me gusta
I don't like.................... No me gusta
I love .... Me gusta mucho
I hate .... Odio
I can't stand................. No aguanto
I prefer.......................... Prefiero
I prefer.......................... Me gusta más

I share your opinion ..... Estoy de acuerdo
I quite agree .... Estoy completamente de acuerdo
I don't agree .... No estoy de acuerdo
You are right .... Tienes razón
You are wrong .... Estás equivocado/a

I think that … .... Creo que …
I think so .... Creo que sí
I don't think so............ No lo creo

I must admit that … ... Debo admitir que …
I don't know................ No sé
It's possible................. Es posible
That depends............... Depende
They say that … .... Se dice que …
perhaps........................ quizás
on the contrary .... al contrario

Justifications

I like it.......................... Me gusta
It's amusing .... Es divertido/a
It's delicious................ Es delicioso/a
It's easy .... Es fácil
It's useful .... Es útil
It's practical .... Es práctico/a
It's fascinating............. Es fascinante
It's interesting .... Es interesante
It interests me.............. Me interesa
It fascinates me .... Me fascina
It makes me laugh .... Me hace reír

I don't like it .... No me gusta
It's annoying .... Es molesto/a
It's awful .... Es malísimo/a
It's a waste of time....... Es una pérdida de tiempo
It's boring.................... Es aburrido/a
It's complicated........... Es complicado/a
It's difficult .... Es difícil
It's disgusting.............. Es repugnante
It's disgusting.............. Es asqueroso/a
It's not worth it .... No merece la pena

It's too big .... Es demasiado grande
It's too complicated...... Es demasiado complicado/a
It's too difficult .... Es demasiado difícil
It's too expensive .... Es demasiado caro/a
It's too far away .... Está demasiado lejos
It's too long .... Es demasiado largo/a
It's too short .... Es demasiado corto/a
It's not practical .... No es práctico/a
It's not possible........... No es posible

It annoys me .... Me molesta
It bores me................... Me aburre
It gets on my nerves ..... Me fastidia
It irritates me .... Me irrita
It makes me tired.......... Me cansa
I haven't any money..... No tengo dinero
I haven't time .... No tengo tiempo
It's unbelievable.......... Es increíble

Miscellaneous

Here is/are .... Aquí tienes/tiene
There is/are .... Hay
There is/are not .... No hay
He is nice .... Es simpático
She is nice .... Es simpática

If you have difficulties …

I'm sorry, I don't understand .... Lo siento, no entiendo
Would you repeat that, please? .... Repite/Repita, por favor
What does that mean? .... ¿Qué significa esto?
Do you speak English/Spanish? .... ¿Habla/Hable inglés/español?
What is that called in Spanish? .... ¿Cómo se llama en español?
How do you say that in Spanish, please? .... ¿Cómo se dice en español?
Speak more slowly, please .... Habla/Hable más despacio, por favor
I've forgotten the word for … .... He olvidado la palabra para …
How do you pronounce that? .... ¿Cómo se pronuncia esto?
How do you spell that, please? .... ¿Cómo se deletrea escribe esto, por favor?
Would you write that for me, please? .... ¿Me lo escribes/escribe, por favor?
Can you explain that, please? .... ¿Puedes/Puede explicarlo, por favor?
Can you help me, please? .... ¿Puedes/Puede ayudarme, por favor?
Will you come with me, please? .... ¿Quieres/Quiere acompañarme, por favor?

Helping someone else

What is the matter? .... ¿Qué pasa?
Have you got/Is there a problem? .... ¿Tienes/Hay algún problema?
Would you like me to help you? .... ¿Quieres/Quiere que te/le ayude?
May I help you? .... ¿Puedo ayudarte/le

Describing things and people

It's a sort of … .... Es un tipo de …
It's a bit like … .... Es un poco como …
It's smaller than … .... Es más pequeño/a que …
It's as big as … .... Es tan grande como …
What does he/she look like? .... ¿Cómo es?
He/She seems older .... Parece más viejo/a
He seems nice .... Parece simpático
She seems unhappy .... No parece contenta
He has black hair and brown eyes .... Tiene el pelo negro y los ojos marrones
She is wearing school uniform .... Lleva uniforme escolar

Instructions you may meet in the Speaking Test

These instructions are given in both *tú* and *usted* forms

Answer the question .... Contesta/Conteste a la pregunta
Ask for the following information .... Pide/Pida la información siguiente
Ask questions .... Haz/Haga preguntas
Describe the picture .... Describe/Describa la ilustración
End the conversation politely .... Termina/Termine la conversación educadamente
Explain .... Explica/Explique
Greet the shopkeeper .... Saluda/Salude al tendero
Greet the examiner .... Saluda/Salude al examinador

Look at the pictures/the photos .... Mira/Mire las ilustraciones/las fotos
Repeat .... Repite/Repita
Speak .... Habla/Hable
Say what you did .... Habla/Hable de lo que hiciste/hizo
Say what you saw .... Habla/Hable de lo que viste/vio
Thank the shopkeeper .... Da/De las gracias al tendero
Use these symbols to make up a dialogue .... Utiliza/Utilice estos símbolos para hacer un diálogo
You are going to answer some questions .... Vas/Va a contestar a unas preguntas

Personal identification

Hello

May I introduce ...? .... ¿Me permites/Me permite presentarte/le a ...?
Pleased to meet you .... Mucho gusto
You know Chris, don't you? .... Conoces/Conoce a Chris ¿No?

What is your first name? .... ¿Cuál es tu/su nombre de pila?
My name is ... . Me llamo ...
What nationality are you? .... ¿Cuál es tu/su nacionalidad?
I am English/British .... Soy inglés/inglesa/británico/británica
I am Irish/Scottish/Welsh .... Soy irlandés/irlandesa/escocés/escocesa/galés/galesa
Where do you come from? .... ¿De dónde eres/es?
I come from London/Edinburgh .... Soy de Londres/Edimburgo
How old are you? .... ¿Cuántos años tienes/tiene?
I am 16 .... Tengo dieciséis años
When is your birthday? .... ¿Cuándo es tu/su cumpleaños?
My birthday is 30th November .... Mi cumpleaños es el treinta de noviembre
What is your date of birth? .... ¿Cuál es la fecha de tu/su nacimiento?
I was born on 21 June 1988 .... Nací el veintiuno de junio de mil novecientos ochenta y ocho
In which year were you born? .... ¿En qué año naciste?
I was born in 1989 .... Nací en mil novecientos ochenta y nueve
Where do you live? .... ¿Dónde vives/vive?
I live in Malvern .... Vivo en Malvern
What is your address? .... ¿Cuál es tu/su dirección?
Write your address in capital letters .... Escribe/Escriba tu/su dirección en mayúsculas
I live at 302, Church Street .... Vivo en la calle Church número trescientos dos
What is your phone number? .... ¿Cuál es tu/su número de teléfono?
My phone number is 57-74-33 .... Mi número de teléfono es el cincuenta y siete, setenta y cuatro, treinta y tres
Have you got a fax number? .... ¿Tienes/tiene número de fax?
What is you email address? .... ¿Cuál es tu/su dirección email?
My email address is .... Mi dirección email es ...
No, sorry, I haven't a fax number .... No, lo siento, no tengo número de fax
How long have you lived in Malvern? .... ¿Desde hace cuánto vives/vive en Malvern?

I have lived there for ten years	Vivo allí desde hace diez años
Have you any brothers or sisters?	¿Tienes/Tiene hermanos o hermanas?
I have one brother. His name is Paul	Tengo un hermano. Se llama Paul
He is older than I am. He is 18	Es mayor que yo. Tiene dieciocho años
I have one sister	Tengo una hermana
She is 13. She is younger than I am	Tiene trece años. Es menor que yo
What does your father do?	¿Qué hace tu/su padre?
What does your mother do?	¿Qué hace tu/su madre?
He is a builder. She is a nurse	Es constructor. Es enfermera
My brother is married	Mi hermano está casado
My sister is single	Mi hermana es soltera
My parents are separated/divorced	Mis padres están separados/divorciados
My mother is a widow	Mi madre es viuda
My father is dead	Mi padre está muerto

Being a guest

Arriving

How are you?	¿Qué tal?/¿Cómo estás/está?
I'm very well, thank you	Muy bien, gracias
How are your parents?	¿Cómo están tus/sus padres?
They are very well, thank you	Muy bien, gracias
And how is your brother?	¿Y tu hermano?
Unfortunately he is ill. He has flu	Desafortunadamente está enfermo. Tiene la gripe
Have you had a good journey?	¿Has/Ha hecho un buen viaje?
The journey was very long	El viaje era muy largo
The crossing was bad/good	La travesía fue mala/buena
I was sea-sick	Estaba mareado/a
I am tired	Estoy cansado/a
Would you like something to eat/drink?	¿Quieres comer/beber algo?
Yes, I'm hungry/I'm thirsty	Sí, tengo hambre/tengo sed
Where is the bathroom?	¿Donde está el cuarto de baño?
The bathroom is on the first floor	El cuarto de baño está en el primer piso
May I have a shower/bath?	¿Puedo ducharme/bañarme?
Here is your room/the bathroom	Aquí está tu habitación/el cuarto de baño
You can put your things in this wardrobe	Puedes poner tus cosas en este armario
Do you need anything?	¿Necesitas algo?
I need some soap, please	Necesito jabón, por favor
I have forgotten my toothbrush	He olvidado mi cepillo de dientes
Can you lend me a flannel?	¿Puedes/Puede prestarme un paño?
Did you sleep well?	¿Has dormido bien?
I slept very well, thank you	Sí, he dormido muy bien, gracias
What do you usually have for breakfast?	¿Qué tomas normalmente para el desayuno?
I have toast and tea	Tomo tostadas y té

Is there anything you don't like to eat?................¿Hay algo que no te gusta comer?
I don't like spinach ....No me gustan las espinacas
Is this your first visit to Spain?............................¿Es tu primera visita en España?
Have you ever been abroad before?.....................¿Has estado en el extranjero antes?
I went on a school visit/exchange last year..........Hice una visita/un intercambio escolar el año pasado
I went to Greece with my parents ....Fui a Grecia con mis padres

In the home

Make yourself at home ....Estás en tu casa
Would you like to listen to cassettes/the radio?...¿Quieres escuchar casetes/la radio?
Would you like to watch TV/a video?.................¿Quieres ver la televisión/un vídeo?
Would you like to borrow my walkman®? ....¿Quieres usar mi walkman®?
Would you like to go out this evening? ....¿Quieres salir esta tarde?
Yes, please ....Sí, por favor
May I help you? ....¿Puedo ayudarte/le?
May I give you a hand?..¿Puedo echarte/le una mano?
Shall we set/clear the table?................................¿Ponemos/Quitamos la mesa?
Will you close the window, please? ....¿Cierras la ventana, por favor?
What is there to be done? ....¿Qué hay que hacer?
I have to tidy up my room....................................Tengo que arreglar mi habitación
I am going to do my homework...........................Voy a hacer mis deberes
Would you like to borrow a book? ....¿Quieres leer un libro?
What is it about?..¿De qué se trata?
Who is it by?...¿Quién lo ha escrito?
I like reading books and magazines.....................Me gusta leer libros y revistas
I don't like reading newspapers...........................No me gusta leer periódicos
May I listen to the radio/watch TV, please?........¿Puedo escuchar la radio/ver la televisión, por favor?
May I phone my parents, please?.........................¿Puedo telefonear a mis padres, por favor?

Goodbye

See you soon/sometime/next year.........................Hasta pronto/luego/el año que viene
Have a good journey home ....Que tengas una buena vuelta a casa
Thank you for everything....................................Muchas gracias por todo
I've had a wonderful holiday...............................He pasado unas vacaciones fenomenales
You have been so kind...Habéis/Han sido todos muy amables
I'll come with you to the station ....Te acompañaré a la estación
You'll phone us when you get home, won't you? .....Nos vas a llamar al llegar a casa, ¿no?
Have you forgotten anything?..............................¿Has olvidado algo?
Have you got everything? ....¿Tienes todo?
Say thank you to your parents for me, please ......Da las gracias a tus padres de mi parte, por favor
Will you be able to come back next year? ....¿Podrás venir otra vez el año que viene?
I'd love to come and see you again......................Me gustaría mucho venir a veros/verles otra vez
Write soon! ....¡Escríbeme pronto!

School

What time do you get up? ....¿A qué hora te levantas?
I get up at 7.00 ....Me levanto a las siete
What time do you leave home in the morning?...¿A qué hora sales de casa por la mañana?
I leave home at 8.15 ....Salgo de casa a las ocho y cuarto
How do you go to school? ....¿Cómo llegas al insti(tuto)?
I go by bus/car/train/bike ....Llego en autobús/coche/tren/bici(cleta)
My brother walks to school.................................Mi hermano llega al insti(tuto) a pie
We live 2 km from school...................................Vivimos a dos kilómetros del insti(tuto)
It takes me 20 minutes to walk ....Llevo veinte minutos andando para llegar al insti(tuto)
What time do you arrive at school? ....¿A qué hora llegas al insti(tuto)?
I arrive at school at 8.35.......................................Llego al insti(tuto) a las nueve menos veinticinco
When do lessons start?...¿A qué hora empiezan las clases?
Lessons start at 9.00...Las clases empiezan a las nueve
When is your lunch time? ....¿A qué hora es la comida?
Lunch time is at 12.30..La comida es a las doce y media
When does school end?..¿A qué hora terminan las clases?
School ends at 3.40 ....Las clases terminan a las cuatro menos veinte
What time do you get home? ....¿A qué hora llegas a casa?
I get home at 4.10...Llego a casa a las cuatro y diez
What time do you go to bed? ....¿A qué hora te acuestas?
I go to bed at 10.30 ....Me acuesto a las diez y media
How many lessons do you have each day? ....¿Cuántas clases tienes al día?
I have six lessons a day.......................................Tengo seis clases al día
How long do your lessons last? ....¿Cuánto tiempo duran las clases?
Our lessons last 50 minutes ....Las clases duran cincuenta minutos
What is your favourite subject? ....¿Cuál es tu asignatura preferida?
My favourite lesson is Spanish ....Mi asignatura preferida es el español
Which subject do you dislike?.............................¿Qué asignatura no te gusta?
I can't stand History...No aguanto la historia
I find German very difficult ....Encuentro muy difícil el alemán
The grammar is difficult ....La gramática es difícil
My sister prefers PE...Mi hermana prefiere la educación física
What do you do during break?............................¿Qué haces durante el recreo?
I talk to my friends during break..........................Durante el recreo charlo con mis amigos
Do you eat in the canteen at midday? ....¿Comes en el comedor del colegio a mediodía?
What do you eat at lunch time?...........................¿Qué comes a mediodía?
I have sandwiches at midday...............................Como bocadillos a mediodía
How many weeks summer holiday do you have? ¿Cuántas semanas de vacaciones tienes?
We have six weeks' holiday in summer ....Tenemos seis semanas de vacaciones en el verano
When do you go back to school? ....¿Cuándo vuelves al insti(tuto)?
We go back on September 6th ....Volvemos el seis de setiembre

Do you have a lot of homework? .... ¿Tienes muchos deberes?
Yes, I think we get too much homework .... Sí, creo que tenemos demasiados deberes
How many hours homework do you do each evening? .... ¿Cuántas horas de deberes haces cada tarde?
I do two hours homework each evening .... Hago dos horas de deberes cada tarde
What do you do in the evening? .... ¿Qué haces por la tarde?
I do my homework and listen to music in the evening .... Hago mis deberes y escucho música por la tarde
Do you help your father/mother prepare the meal? .... ¿Ayudas a tu/su padre/madre a preparar la comida?
No, but I have to do the washing up .... No, pero tengo que fregar los platos
Do you watch TV in the evening? .... ¿Ves la televisión por la tarde?
Yes, sometimes .... Sí, a veces

Part-time jobs, work experience and pocket money

Do you have a Saturday job? .... ¿Trabajas los sábados?
Yes, I work on Saturday .... Sí, trabajo los sábados
Where do you work? .... ¿Dónde trabajas?
I work in a shop .... Trabajo en una tienda
What is your job? .... ¿Qué trabajo tienes?
I am a sales assistant .... Soy dependiente/dependienta
When do you start work in the morning? .... ¿A qué hora empiezas por la mañana?
I start at 8.00 am .... Empiezo a las ocho
I work seven hours every Saturday .... Trabajo siete horas cada sábado
How much do you earn an hour? .... ¿Cuánto ganas por hora?
I earn … per hour .... Gano … por hora
What time do you finish work? .... ¿A qué hora terminas el trabajo?
I finish work at 4.30 .... Termino a las cuatro y media
I go babysitting for neighbours .... Hago de canguro para los vecinos
Last year I did work experience in a factory .... El año pasado hice prácticas laborales en una fábrica
I don't have a Saturday job .... No trabajo los sábados
My parents give me £ / €… pocket money each week .... Mis padres me dan … (libras/euros) para mis gastos cada semana
What do you do with your money? .... ¿Qué haces con tu dinero?
I am saving up for a computer .... Estoy ahorrando para un ordenador
I like buying clothes/books/computer games ...... Me gusta comprar ropa/libros/juegos electrónicos

Shopping

You will say:

Is there a post-office near here? .... ¿Hay una oficina de correos por aquí?
Which is the way to the bank, please? .... ¿Por dónde se va al banco, por favor?
Do you sell …? .... ¿Venden …?
May we look round? .... ¿Podemos mirar?
I'm just looking .... Estoy mirando solamente

Please could you tell me where I can buy …? .....¿Puede Vd. decirme dónde puedo comprar …?
I would prefer..Preferiría

Paying:

How much is it? ....¿Cuánto es?
How much do I owe you? ....¿Cuánto le debo?
Do I have to pay at the till?.................................¿Hay que pagar en la caja?
May I pay by credit card/cheque? ....¿Puedo pagar con tarjeta de crédito/cheque?
Do you take cheques? ....¿Aceptan cheques?
Have you got change for 20 euros?......................¿Tiene Vd. cambio de veinte euros?
I've only got a 50 euro note ....Sólo tengo un billete de cincuenta euros

You will hear:

Who is next? ....¿Quién es el siguiente?
May I help you? ....¿En qué puedo servirle?
Anything else? ....¿Algo más?
We haven't got any ....No tenemos/No hay
Is that all?...¿Eso es todo?
Have you got any change? ....¿Tiene Vd. cambio?
What is your size? (Clothes)................................¿Qué talla tiene Vd.?
What size do you take? (Shoes)...........................¿Qué número calza Vd.?

Food

Have you any bread/meat/olive oil/eggs? ....¿Tiene pan/carne/aceite/huevos?
Have you got a small packet of coffee? ....¿Tiene Vd. un paquete pequeño de café?
I would like three peaches, please........................Quisiera tres melocotones, por favor
Give me a kilo of potatoes, please ....Deme un kilo de patatas, por favor
I'll take two tins of sardines................................Voy a llevarme dos latas de sardinas
I'd like 250 grammes of chocolate.......................Quisiera doscientos cincuenta gramos de chocolate
No thank you, I won't take that - it's too dear .....No, gracias, no voy a llevarme eso - es demasiado caro/a

Amounts and quantities

100 grammes of … ....Cien gramos de …
500 grammes of cherries.....................................Quinientos gramos de cerezas
A kilo of apples...Un kilo de manzanas
A bottle of … ....Una botella de …
A jar of … ....Un bote de …
A packet/tin/box of biscuits ....Un paquete/Una lata/Una caja de galletas
A piece of cake..Un trozo de pastel
A slice of ham ....Una loncha de jamón
The oranges are 30 cents each.............................Las naranjas son a treinta céntimos cada una

Clothes

What size is it?	¿Qué talla tiene?
I am size 14	Tengo la talla 36
How much does that jumper cost?	¿Cuánto cuesta ese jersey?
Do you have it in a different colour?	¿Lo/La tiene Vd. en otro color?
May I try on the blue skirt, please?	¿Me puedo probar la falda azul, por favor?
It's too big (small, tight, expensive)	Es demasiado grande (pequeño/a, estrecho/a, caro/a)
Have you got anything cheaper?	¿Tiene Vd. algo más barato?
I'll take these socks	Voy a quedarme con estos calcetines
I like the colour	Me gusta el color

Shoes

Where is the shoe department, please?	¿Dónde está la sección de zapatos, por favor?
I would like to try on these black shoes, please	Quiero probarme estos zapatos negros, por favor
I take size 6	Calzo el número 39
They are too tight	Son demasiado estrechos
I prefer the blue sandals	Prefiero las sandalias azules

Presents and souvenirs

Have you got any postcards, please?	¿Tiene tarjetas postales?
Do you sell films?	¿Venden películas?
What is the price of this book, please?	¿Cuál es el precio de este libro, por favor?
I would like to buy a black leather handbag	Quisiera comprar un bolso de cuero negro
May I see the bag which is in the window on the left?	¿Puedo ver el bolso que está en el escaparate a la izquierda?
It's for a present	Es para un regalo
Will you gift-wrap it, please?	¿Me lo envuelve, por favor?

Problems

I think there is a mistake	Creo que hay un error
The colour does not suit me	No me va el color
I have kept the receipt	He guardado el recibo
I would like to change this bag	Quiero cambiar este bolso
I followed the washing instructions, but this jumper has shrunk	Seguí las instrucciones de lavado, pero este jersey (se) ha encogido
Excuse me, these shoes are not the same size	Perdone/Perdóneme, estos zapatos no son del mismo tamaño

Eating and drinking

In a café

Could you tell me the way to the Café Altamira, please?	¿Por dónde se va al Café Altamira, por favor?
I've promised to meet my penfriend there	He quedado con mi amigo allí
Let's go for a drink	Vamos a tomar una copita
I'll buy you a drink	Te voy a invitar a una copita

I'm paying .... Te invito yo
Waiter! .... ¡Oiga, camarero!
Waitress! .... ¡Oiga, camarera!
What will you have? .... ¿Qué vas/va a tomar?
What would you like to drink? .... ¿Qué quieres/quiere beber?
Do you wish to order? .... ¿Quieres/quiere pedir?
I would like a bottle of lemonade, please .... Quisiera una botella de limonada, por favor
I would like a beer, please .... Quiero una cerveza, por favor
Anything else? .... ¿Algo más?
Have you got any crisps, please? .... ¿Tiene Vd. patatas fritas, por favor?
Do you sell sandwiches? .... ¿Venden bocadillos?
What sort of sandwiches do have you? .... ¿Qué bocadillos hay?
Have you got any cheese sandwiches, please? ..... ¿Tiene Vd. bocadillos de queso, por favor?
How much is a ham sandwich? .... ¿Cuánto es un bocadillo de jamón?
How much do I owe you? .... ¿Cuánto le debo?
Is the service charge included? .... ¿El servicio está incluido?

In a restaurant

Have you got a table for four? .... ¿Tiene Vd. una mesa para cuatro personas?
What name is it? .... ¿A que nombre?
I've reserved a table in the name of Robert .... He reservado una mesa a nombre de Robert
I'd like a table near the window/on the terrace .... Quiero una mesa cerca de la ventana/en la terraza
I'd like to see the menu, please .... Quiero ver el menú, por favor
What do you recommend? .... ¿Qué recomienda Vd.?
I recommend the fish .... Recomiendo el pescado
Today's set meal is … .... El menú del día es …
I'll have the 20 euro meal .... Voy a tomar el menú de veinte euros
Have you decided? .... ¿Han decidido?
I'd like to order now .... Quiero pedir ahora
To start with, I'll have tomato salad .... Para empezar, voy a tomar ensalada de tomate
For the main course, I'd like steak and chips .... Como plato principal, quiero biftec con patatas fritas
What sort of vegetables do you have? .... ¿Qué verduras tienen?
I like mushrooms .... Me gustan los champiñones
I won't have spinach; I don't like spinach .... No voy a tomar espinacas; no me gustan las espinacas
I'll have peas and carrots, please .... Voy a tomar guisantes y zanahorias, por favor
For dessert I'll have ice cream .... De postre voy a tomar helado
Which flavours do you have? .... ¿Qué sabores hay?
I prefer chocolate ice cream .... Prefiero helado de chocolate
I'll have mineral water to drink .... Para beber, voy a tomar agua mineral
May I have the bill, please .... La cuenta, por favor

Difficulties

We need another fork...Necesitamos otro tenedor
I ordered 20 minutes ago ....Pedí hace veinte minutos
That's not what I ordered....................................No es lo que pedí
You have brought vanilla ice cream,but ....Ha traído un helado de vainilla, pero
I ordered a chocolate ice cream pedí un helado de chocolate
We would like some sugar, please........................Queremos azúcar, por favor
The meat is overdone...La carne está demasiado hecha
Please will you change this glass.........................Hágame el favor de cambiar este vaso, por favor
I think there is a mistake in the bill......................Creo que hay un error en la cuenta

Services

At the bank

Which is the counter for changing money? ....¿Dónde está la ventanilla de cambio de dinero?
I would like to change some travellers' cheques . .....Quisiera cambiar unos cheques de viaje
Is there a commission?...¿Hay comisión?
What is the exchange rate for the pound?............¿Cuál es el tipo de cambio de la libra esterlina?
Have you got any means of identification?..........¿Tiene Vd. alguna documentación?
May I see your passport? ....¿Puedo ver su pasaporte?
Do I have to sign?..¿Tengo que firmar?
Would you sign, please..¿Quiere Vd. firmar, por favor?
Where do I have to sign? ....¿Dónde tengo que firmar?
What is today's date?..¿Qué fecha es hoy?
May I borrow a pen, please?................................¿Me da/deja un bolígrafo, por favor?
What time does the bank open/close?..................¿A qué hora se abre/cierra el banco?
Where is there a cashpoint? ....¿Dónde puedo encontrar un cajero automático?

At the Post Office

How much does it cost to send a letter to the UK?....¿Cuánto cuesta mandar una carta al Reino Unido?
I would like to send this parcel to the UK ....Quisiera mandar este paquete al Reino Unido
How long will it take? ....¿Cuánto tiempo tarda en llegar?
Letters usually take three days ....Las cartas tardan tres días normalmente
Six stamps, please...Seis sellos, por favor
Where is the letter box?.......................................¿Dónde está el buzón?
Over there, next to the phone box........................Está allí, al lado de la cabina telefónica
I'd like to send a telegram....................................Quisiera poner un telegrama
How much is it per word?....................................¿Cuánto es por palabra?
What time is the next collection? ....¿A qué hora es la próxima recogida?
Is the post office open on Saturday morning? .....¿La oficina de correos está abierta los sábados por la mañana?
Will you weigh this parcel, please? ....¿Quiere pesar este paquete, por favor?
Is there a letter for me, please? ....¿Por favor, hay una carta para mí?
What is your name? ....¿Cómo se llama?
My name is … ....Me llamo …

Have you got any means of identification?..........¿Tiene Vd. alguna documentación?
Here is my passport...Aquí tiene mi pasaporte

Using the phone

Hello, Anne speaking..Dígame, soy Anne
This is the Melero's house..................................Esta es la casa de la familia Melero
I am Miguel's English penfriend ....Soy el amigo inglés/la amiga inglesa de Miguel
Is Miguel there? ....¿Está Miguel?
Everyone's out. Can I take a message?................Todo el mundo ha salido. ¿Quieres dejar un recado?
It's the first time I've used a phone in Spain ....Es la primera vez que utilizo el teléfono en España
Say that again, please...¿Puede repetirlo, por favor?
Will you spell that, please?.................................¿Puede deletrear eso, por favor?
You are wanted on the phone..............................Te/Le llaman al teléfono
Can I use the phone box outside the Post Office? .....¿Puedo utilizar el teléfono fuera de Correos?
Is it a card phone? ....¿Es un teléfono de tarjeta?
Do you sell phone cards? ....¿Venden tarjetas telefónicas?
I would like a 50 unit card ....Quiero una tarjeta de cincuenta unidades
Can I phone from here?.......................................¿Puedo telefonear desde aquí?
Can you get me 57-74-33, please.........................Póngame con el cincuenta y siete, setenta y cuatro, treinta y tres, por favor
What is your phone number? ....¿Cuál es tu/su número de teléfono?
Do you know the code?..¿Conoces/Conoce el prefijo?
What is the code for London?.............................¿Cuál es el prefijo para Londres?
Our phone number is 57-74-33............................Nuestro número de teléfono es el cincuenta y siete, setenta y cuatro, treinta y tres
Have you got a mobile? ....¿Tienes/Tiene móvil?
Where are the directories? ....¿Dónde están las guías telefónicas?
You must phone Directory Enquiries...................Hay que llamar a información
Can you tell me the number of the hospital, please?............................¿Puede Vd. decirme el número de teléfono del hospital?
I would like to reverse the charges.......................Quiero llamar a cobro revertido
I've been cut off ....Me han desconectado
Hold the line...Espere/No cuelgue
I need to phone the UK ....Tengo que llamar al Reino Unido
What must I do, please?.......................................¿Qué tengo que hacer, por favor?
To ring UK, dial 0044, then the area code ....Para llamar al Reino Unido marque el 0044, luego
without the 0, and then the number of the ....el prefijo de la región sin el cero, y luego el número
person you are ringing..de la persona a quién llama

The workplace

Phoning at work

Is Señora Ortega available today?........................¿La señora Ortega está disponible hoy?
May I speak to the Personnel Manager, please? ..¿Puedo hablar con el jefe de personal?
I have an appointment with the Personnel Manager..Tengo una cita con el jefe de personal

I saw your advert in the paper	Vi su anuncio en el periódico
Can you send me a job application form, please?	¿Puede enviarme un impreso de solicitud, por favor?
I would like to speak to …	Quisiera hablar con …
Can you put me through to …, please?	¿Puede ponerme con …, por favor?
Do you know his/her extension?	¿Conoce su número de extensión?
I would like to make an appointment with …	Quiero hacer una cita con …
Who is speaking?	¿Quién habla?
Can you wait?	¿Puede esperar?
He is in a meeting	Está en una reunión
When can I speak to him?	¿Cuándo puedo hablar con él?
I phoned, but it was engaged	Llamé, pero estaba comunicando
Can you ring back?	¿Puede volver a llamar?
What time shall I ring back?	¿A qué hora vuelvo a llamar?
I'll ring back at midday	Volveré a llamar a mediodía
May I leave a message?	¿Puedo dejar un recado?
Please tell Sra. Ortega that Sr. Ruiz called	Por favor, dígale a la señora Ortega que el señor Ruiz ha llamado
May I take a message for him/her?	¿Quiere dejar un recado para él/ella?
Can we arrange a meeting?	¿Podemos acordar una cita?
Can you fax me a message?	¿Puede enviarme una nota por fax?
My fax number is …	Mi número de fax es …
Can you send me an email, please?	¿Puede enviarme un mensaje por correo electrónico?
My email address is …	Mi dirección de correo electrónico es …
Can you send me an email, please?	¿Quiere enviarme un córreo electrónico, por favor?
My email address is …	Mi dirección email es …

Applying for a job

Where is the Job Centre, please?	¿Dónde está la oficina de empleo, por favor?
I want to find a job	Quiero encontrar un trabajo
I'm looking for a part-time job	Busco un trabajo por horas
Where do you come from?	¿De dónde eres?
I come from Bromsgrove	Soy de Bromsgrove
Are you staying long in Spain?	¿Te vas/Se va a quedar mucho tiempo en España?
Yes, I'm staying for six weeks	Sí, me voy a quedar seis semanas
What work have you done before?	¿Qué trabajo has/ha hecho antes?
I've worked in a supermarket	He trabajado en un supermercado
Why did you decide to apply for this job?	¿Por qué decidiste/decidió solicitar este trabajo?
It interests me	Me interesa
Have you any experience of office work?	¿Tienes/Tiene alguna experiencia de trabajo de oficina?
What sort of work experience have you done?	¿Qué ha hecho como prácticas laborales?
I did work experience in an office	Hice prácticas en una oficina
Are you computer-literate?	¿Sabes/Sabe de informática?

Yes, I have a computer at home .... Sí, tengo un ordenador en casa

What languages have you studied, besides Spanish? .... ¿Qué idiomas has/ha estudiado, aparte del español?

I have studied German/French .... He estudiado (el) alemán/(el) francés

Are you willing to work on Saturday? .... ¿Estás/Está dispuesto/a a trabajar los sábados

Yes, certainly. .... Sí, por supuesto

Can you give me details about the job? .... ¿Puede darme detalles sobre el empleo?

You will deal with the post .... Te ocuparás/Se ocupará del correo

You will have to do the filing .... Tendrás/Tendrá que archivar documentos

When can you start? .... ¿Cuándo puedes/puede empezar?

I can start whenever you wish .... Puedo empezar cuando quiera

Will you fill in the form, please? .... ¿Quieres/Quiere rellenar el formulario, por favor?

Holidays

At the tourist office

What should we see in the town? .... ¿Qué debemos ver en la ciudad?

Do you do guided tours of the town? .... ¿Hay visitas con guía de la ciudad?

I would like a town plan, please .... Quiero un plano de la ciudad, por favor

Have you got a map of the area? .... ¿Tiene Vd. un mapa de la región?

Can you give me a list of campsites? .... ¿Puede darme una lista de campings?

Can you recommend a good hotel/ restaurant in the town? .... ¿Puede recomendarme un buen hotel/ restaurante en la ciudad?

We are only spending three days here .... Vamos a pasar sólo tres días aquí

Have you any brochures about the cathedral? ...... ¿Tiene folletos sobre la catedral?

When is the museum open? .... ¿Cuándo está abierto el museo?

Is it closed on Tuesdays? .... ¿Está cerrado los martes?

Do you have to pay to go in? .... ¿Hay que pagar para entrar?

Where is the bus station? .... ¿Dónde está la estación de autobuses?

May I have a bus timetable, please? .... ¿Puede darme un horario de autobuses, por favor?

Can one go for trips to the seaside? .... ¿Se puede ir de excursión a la playa?

Where can I hire a car/bike? .... ¿Dónde puedo alquilar un coche/una bici(cleta)?

Have you got information about other parts of Spain? .... ¿Tiene información sobre otras partes de España?

I like visiting castles/churches .... Me gusta visitar los castillos/las iglesias

I have never been there .... No he estado nunca allí

Can I get there by train? .... ¿Se puede ir allí en tren?

Do I have to go on to the motorway? .... ¿Hay que ir por la autopista?

Where do I get onto it? .... ¿Dónde empalmo con la autopista?

Which exit is it? .... ¿Qué salida es?

It's exit 9 .... Es la salida número nueve

At the hotel

Have you got any rooms available?	¿Tiene alguna habitación?
No, I'm sorry, the hotel is full	No, lo siento, el hotel está completo
Is there another hotel nearby?	¿Hay otro hotel cerca de aquí?
I have reserved a room in the name of Robert	He reservado una habitación a nombre de Robert
I phoned you two days ago	Le llamé hace dos días
I sent you a fax yesterday	Le envié un fax ayer
No, I am not Mr X, I am Mr Y	No, no soy el señor X, soy el señor Y
I would like a single room	Quisiera una habitación individual
I would like a double room	Quisiera una habitación doble
with a double bed/with twin beds	con cama de matrimonio/con dos camas
with bathroom/shower	con baño/ducha
For how long?/For how many nights?	¿Por cuánto tiempo?/¿Para cuántas noches?
We shall be staying for four nights	Vamos a quedarnos cuatro noches
What is the price per person/per night?	¿Cuánto es por persona/por noche?
Is breakfast included?	¿Está incluido el desayuno?
May I have the key to my room, please?	¿Puede darme la llave de mi habitación?
Here is the key for room 108	Aquí tiene la llave de la habitación número ciento ocho
Is there a car-park?	¿Hay aparcamiento?
You can park behind the hotel	Se puede aparcar detrás del hotel
Parking is not allowed in front of the hotel	Está prohibido aparcar delante del hotel
When is breakfast?	¿A qué hora es el desayuno?
You can have breakfast between 7.00 and 10.00 am	El desayuno es entre las siete y las diez de la mañana
At what time is dinner served?	¿A qué hora se sirve la cena?
Dinner is served from 8.00 until 10.00 pm	Se sirve la cena de las ocho hasta las diez de la noche
Is there a lift? Does the lift work?	¿Hay ascensor? ¿Funciona el ascensor?
Does the hotel have a restaurant?	¿Hay un restaurante en el hotel?
I'm sorry, we do not have a restaurant	Lo siento, no hay restaurante
There is a very good restaurant on the corner	Hay un restaurante muy bueno en la esquina
May I have towels and soap for Room 108, please	¿Puede darme toallas y jabón para la habitación número ciento ocho, por favor
There are no coathangers in Room 108	No hay perchas en la habitación número 108
I have lost the key to my room	He perdido la llave de mi habitación
I'm sorry, but I have broken the lamp	Lo siento, pero he roto la lámpara
We could not sleep because of the traffic noise	No pudimos dormir a causa del ruido del tráfico
We would like to change rooms, please	Queremos cambiar de habitación, por favor
Please can someone bring up my cases?	Por favor, quiero que suban mis maletas
May I have the bill, please?	La cuenta, por favor

At the youth hostel

Where is the nearest youth hostel?	¿Dónde está el albergue juvenil más cercano?
May I see the warden, please?	¿Puedo ver al guardián, por favor?
Do you have any beds available for tonight?	¿Hay camas disponibles para esta noche?
There are three of us, two girls and one boy	Somos tres, dos chicas y un chico
How much is it per night?	¿Cuánto es por noche?
How much is breakfast/evening meal?	¿Cuánto es el desayuno/la cena?
Can I hire a sleeping bag?	¿Puedo alquilar un saco de dormir?
Where is the boys'/girls' dormitory, please?	¿Dónde está el dormitorio de los chicos/las chicas?
The girls' dormitory is on the first floor	El dormitorio de las chicas está en el primer piso
The TV room/day room/ games room is on the ground floor	La sala de televisión/el salón/ la sala de juegos está en la planta baja
What time do we have to be back at night?	¿A qué hora tenemos que regresar por la noche?

At the camp site

Have you got room for a tent ?	¿Hay sitio para una tienda?
Have you a pitch for a caravan, please?	¿Hay una plaza para una caravana, por favor?
How long do you plan to stay?	¿Cuánto tiempo piensa Vd. quedarse?
We would like to stay until Saturday/ four nights in all	Quisiéramos quedarnos hasta el sábado/ cuatro noches en total
I would like to be near the swimming pool	Quisiera estar cerca de la piscina
I do not like being under trees	No me gusta estar debajo de los árboles
How many people are there?	¿Cuántas personas hay?
There are four of us, 2 adults and 2 children	Somos cuatro, dos adultos y dos niños
Is there half-price for children?	¿Los niños pagan la mitad?
Is there a shop on site?	¿Hay tienda de comestibles en el camping?
The toilet block is by the trees	Los servicios están cerca de los árboles
The dustbins are behind the toilet block	Los cubos de la basura están detrás de los servicios
Is there an electric connection for caravans?	¿Hay tomas de electricidad para las caravanas?
Where can I get bottles of Camping Gaz®?	¿Dónde se pueden conseguir las botellas de Camping Gaz®?
Is there a play area for the children?	¿Hay un parque para los niños?
Can we get take-away meals on site?	¿Se pueden comprar en el camping comidas para llevar?
The shower is not working	No funciona la ducha
We have no electricity	No tenemos electricidad
May we have a barbecue?	¿Podemos hacer una barbacoa?

Travel and transport

By train

Where is the nearest station?	¿Dónde está la estación más cercana?
How far is that?	¿A qué distancia está de aquí?
Where is that exactly?	¿Dónde está exactamente?
What time does the train leave for Madrid?	¿A qué hora sale el tren para Madrid?

When/At what time does it arrive there?	¿Cuándo/A qué hora llega allí?
Which platform does the train go from?	¿De qué andén sale el tren?
Is it a through train?	¿Es un tren directo?
Do I have to change?	¿Hay que hacer transbordo?
When does the train from Toledo arrive?	¿A qué hora llega el tren de Toledo?
A single ticket to Toledo, please	Un billete de ida para Toledo, por favor
A second class return to Seville, please	Un billete de ida y vuelta de segunda clase para Sevilla, por favor
When does the next train for Burgos leave?	¿A qué hora sale el próximo tren para Burgos?
Is there a train this morning/about 3.00 pm/ this evening?	¿Hay un tren esta mañana/a eso de las tres/ está tarde?
I'd like to reserve a seat	Quisiera reservar una plaza
I'd like a seat near the window	Quisiera una plaza cerca de la ventana
How long does the journey take?	¿Cuánto tiempo dura el viaje?
The journey takes about two hours	El viaje dura dos horas, más o menos
How much does a first class ticket cost?	¿Cuánto cuesta un billete de primera clase?
How long will I have to wait?	¿Cuánto tiempo tengo que esperar?
Will the train arrive on time?	¿Será puntual el tren?
The train will be an hour late because of track repairs	El tren llevará una hora de retraso a causa de las reparaciones en la vía
You have missed the train	Ha perdido Vd. el tren
It left ten minutes ago	Salió hace diez minutos
It is already 10 past 9	Ya son las nueve y diez
It is not yet 10.30	Todavía no son las diez y media
The clock is right	El reloj está en hora
The clock is fast/slow	El reloj se adelanta/se retrasa/está adelantado/retrasado

By plane

When does the next plane for Berlin leave?	¿A qué hora sale el próximo vuelo para Berlin?
Is there a flight to Madrid today/this morning/ this evening?	¿Hay un vuelo para Madrid hoy/por la mañana/ esta tarde?
I'd like a seat in the non-smoking section	Quisiera una plaza de no fumadores
A tourist class ticket	Un billete de clase turista
I would like to leave this morning	Quiero salir esta mañana
There are no more seats available	No quedan plazas
I'd like to change flights	Quiero cambiar de vuelo
Is there a coach to the airport?	¿Hay un autobús hasta el aeropuerto?
Can you confirm the arrival time of the plane from London?	¿Puede Vd. confirmar la hora de llegada del vuelo de Londres?
Can you confirm the departure time of the plane to Madrid?	¿Puede Vd. confirmar la hora de salida del vuelo para Madrid?
The flight has been delayed	El vuelo lleva retraso
It took off an hour late	Despegó con una hora de retraso
Where are my cases?	¿Dónde están mis maletas?

I checked them in at Heathrow ....Las facturé en Heathrow
Where is the duty-free shop? ....¿Dónde está la tienda libre de impuestos/ el "Duty-free"?

By bus/metro/tram

Where is the bus stop? ....¿Dónde está la parada de autobuses?
A multi-journey card, please ....Un bonobús, por favor
Don't forget to stamp your ticket ....No se olvide de picar el billete
The bus was half an hour late because of the fog/snow ....El autobús llevaba media hora de retraso a causa de la niebla/nieve
How often do the buses run? ....¿Cuántos autobuses hay por hora?
I've been waiting 20 minutes already ....Ya llevo veinte minutos esperando
What time is the first/last bus? ....¿A qué hora es el primer/último autobús?
Is this the right bus for the town centre? ....¿Es este el autobús para el centro de la ciudad?
You get off at the town hall ....Bájese al Ayuntamiento
Have I missed the last bus? ....¿He perdido el último autobús?
The nearest tube station is by the theatre ....La estación de metro más cercana está cerca del teatro
Which line do I have to take? ....¿Qué línea debo tomar/coger?
You change here/at the next station ....Cambie Vd. aquí/en la próxima estación
Are there any seats? ....¿Hay asientos libres?
This seat is taken ....Este asiento está ocupado
The underground is very convenient ....El metro es muy práctico

By taxi

Would you like to phone for a taxi? ....¿Quiere Vd. llamar un taxi?
I haven't got the fare for a taxi ....No tengo el precio de un taxi
Where is the taxi rank, please? ....¿Dónde está la parada de taxis, por favor?
How much would it cost to go to the airport? ......¿Cuánto costaría ir al aeropuerto?
How long does the journey take? ....¿Cuánto tiempo dura el viaje?
Will you come for me at 9.00 tomorrow? ....¿Puede venir a recogerme mañana a las nueve?

On the boat

Do you want to go on deck? ....¿Quiere Vd. subir a la cubierta?
I've lost my landing card ....He perdido mi tarjeta de desembarco
I feel seasick! ....¡Estoy mareado/a!

At the garage

Do you do repairs? ....¿Hace Vd. reparaciones?
My car has broken down ....Mi coche está averiado
I've run out of petrol ....Me he quedado sin gasolina
I've got a puncture ....Tengo un pinchazo
The engine won't start ....El motor no arranca/no quiere arrancar
The brakes/The lights are not working ....Los frenos/Los faros no funcionan
The battery is flat ....La batería está descargada
What make of car is it? ....¿Qué marca de coche es?

What is your registration number? ....¿Cuál es la matrícula?/¿Qué matrícula es?
Where are you exactly?..¿Dónde está Vd. exactamente?
I'm on the N634, 5 kilometres from Llanes.........Estoy en la N634, a unos cinco kilómetros de Llanes

At the petrol station

30 litres of unleaded/super unleaded, please ....Treinta litros de sin plomo/súper sin plomo, por favor
Fill it up, please ....Lleno, por favor/Llénelo, por favor
Please check the oil/water...................................Compruebe el aceite/el agua, por favor
Please check the battery/the tyres ....Compruebe la batería/los neumáticos, por favor
Will you reverse, please?.....................................Dé marcha atrás, por favor
Will you switch the engine off, please?..............Pare el motor, por favor
Do you take credit cards?....................................¿Aceptan tarjetas de crédito?
Are there any toilets here? ....¿Hay servicios aquí?
Do you sell maps/town plans/drinks?.................¿Se venden mapas/planos de la ciudad/bebidas?
Over there by the cash desk/toilets ....Allí, cerca de la caja/los servicios
Is it self-service? ....¿Es autoservicio?
One of your tyres is soft.......................................Tiene Vd. un neumático desinflado
I would like to pump up the tyres ....Quisiera inflar los neumáticos

Hiring a bicycle

I would like to hire a bike, please ....Quisiera alquilar una bicicleta, por favor
a touring bike ....una bicicleta de paseo
a mountain bike ....una bicicleta de montaña
Is there a repair kit with the bike? ....¿Tiene la bicicleta caja de herramientas?
You have to pay 80 euros deposit........................Hay que pagar ochenta euros de depósito
Will you fill in this form, please? ....¿Quiere rellenar este impreso, por favor?
How long do you want the bikes?........................¿Cuánto tiempo quieren las bicicletas?
for three days ....tres días

Asking directions

How do I get to the cathedral, please?................¿Por dónde se va a la catedral, por favor?
Where is the station, please?...............................¿Dónde está la estación, por favor?
How long will it take? ....¿Cuánto tiempo lleva?
Are you walking or in a car?...............................¿Va Vd. en coche o a pie?
It will take twenty minutes on foot ....Lleva veinte minutos a pie
Is there a hotel near here? ....¿Hay un hotel cerca de aquí?
Is it far?..¿Está lejos?
Turn left at the traffic lights................................Tuerza a la izquierda en el semáforo
It's on your right after the library.........................Está a la derecha después de la biblioteca
Go straight on as far as the roundabout ....Siga todo derecho hasta la rotonda
Cross the road ....Cruce la carretera/el camino/la calle
Go up/down the road ....Suba/Baje la calle
Go along the road..Siga por la calle

Follow this road till you get to the town hall.......Siga esta calle hasta el Ayuntamiento
Take the first/second/third on the right...............Tome la primera/segunda/tercera (bocacalle) a la derecha
It is a large building near the sea..........................Es un edificio grande cerca del mar
You can get there by bus/tram/metro..................Se puede llegar allí en autobús/tranvía/metro
You'll have to take a taxi....................................Hay/Tendrás que tomar un taxi
It's thirty kilometres from here...........................Está a treinta kilómetros de aquí
Opposite the bank ....Enfrente del banco
On the right of the cinema ....A la derecha del cine
To the left of the park..A la izquierda del parque
Beside the lake ....Al lado del lago
Between the chemist's and the supermarket........Entre la farmacia y el supermercado
At the end of the corridor....................................Al final del pasillo
On the first/second/top floor ....En el primer/segundo/último piso
It's near to the old house with a red roof ....Está cerca de la casa vieja con un tejado rojo

Invitations and outings

Making arrangements

What would you like to do this evening?............¿Qué quieres hacer esta tarde?
Shall we go out this evening? ....¿Por qué no salimos esta tarde?
Where would you like to go?...............................¿Adónde te gustaría ir?
Can we go to the cinema?...................................¿Podemos ir al cine?
What time shall we meet?...................................¿A qué hora nos encontramos?
I'll see you at 8.00 pm..Te veo a las ocho
Where shall we meet?..¿Dónde nos encontramos?
I'll see you outside the restaurant........................Te veo en la puerta del restaurante
Shall we stay in? ....¿Nos quedamos en casa?
Can we hire a video?..¿Podemos alquilar un vídeo?
Have you seen *Harry Potter*? ....¿Has visto *Harry Potter*?
Is it out on video?...¿Ya está en vídeo?
Shall we go for a drink?.......................................¿Vamos a tomar una copita?
I'm paying!...¡Pago yo!

Accepting and refusing

Yes, I'd love to..Sí, me gustaría mucho
I'd love to ....Con mucho gusto
OK, agreed ....Vale, de acuerdo
Of course...Claro
Certainly..Por supuesto
Thank you ....Gracias
It depends ....Depende
I'm not sure ....No estoy seguro/a
I don't know ....No sé
I must ask my penfriend.......................................Debo preguntar a mi amigo/a

I'm sorry, I can't make it ....Lo siento, no puedo
I've got too much homework...............................Tengo demasiados deberes
I haven't got time...No tengo tiempo
Perhaps we could go tomorrow ....Quizás podemos ir mañana
Unfortunately, I'm already doing something.......Desafortunadamente, ya estoy haciendo algo
Sorry, I'm not free..Lo siento, no estoy libre
Sorry, but I have to babysit for some friends.......Lo siento, pero tengo que hacer de canguro para unos amigos

At the cinema

How about going to the cinema? ....¿Por qué no vamos al cine?
What's on?..¿Qué película estrenan/ponen?
I've already seen it...Ya la he visto
I'd like to see a comedy/horror film ....Me gustaría ver una película cómica/de terror
Is it in English? ....¿Es en inglés?
Is it the original soundtrack?...............................¿Es en versión original?
No, it's dubbed ....No, está doblada
Yes, but it's got sub-titles ....Sí, pero hay subtítulos
What time does the last performance start?.........¿A qué hora empieza la última sesión?
How long does it last? ....¿Cuánto tiempo dura?
What time does the film end? ....¿A qué hora termina la película?

Booking a ticket

Can I book seats?...¿Se pueden reservar entradas?
Are there reductions for students? ....¿Hay reducción/descuento para los estudiantes?
Can I buy a student ticket?...................................¿Puedo comprar una entrada de estudiante?
How much is it in the balcony/stalls? ....¿Cuánto es en el entresuelo/el patio de butacas?
Two tickets for the balcony, please ....Dos entradas de entresuelo, por favor
Shall I give the usherette a tip? ....¿Hay que dar una propina a la acomodadora?

Discussing the show

What did you think of the film/play?..................¿Qué te pareció la película?
The film was marvellous/interesting ....La película fue maravillosa/interesante
The concert was boring/awful..............................El concierto fue aburrido/fatal
In my opinion it was too long/serious..................En mi opinión fue demasiado largo/serio
Did you see Antonio Banderas' latest film? ....¿Has visto la última película de Antonio Banderas?
the part played by Russell Crowe ....el papel de Russell Crowe
Who is your favourite singer?..............................¿Quién es tu cantante preferido/a?
My favourite singer is ... .Mi cantante preferido/a es ...
Who is your favourite actor/actress? ....¿Quién es tu actor preferido/actriz preferida?
Which group do you like best? ....¿Qué grupo te gusta más?
I like ... best...Me gusta ... más/Me gustan ... más

Going to a party

Pablo's having a party next week ....Pablo organiza una fiesta en casa la semana que viene

What time does it start? ....¿A qué hora empieza?

It starts at 9.15...Empieza a las nueve y cuarto

Will you come with me to the party on Friday evening? ....¿Quieres venir conmigo a la fiesta el viernes por la tarde?

Sorry, I'm going with John/Emma.......................Lo siento, pero voy con John/Emma

Going to a disco

Are you going to the disco this evening?.............¿Vas a la disco(teca) esta tarde?

Yes, I'd love to..Sí, me encantaría

I'll buy the tickets ....Compraré las entradas

Can I bring a friend? ....¿Puedo invitar a un amigo/una amiga?

Sorry, but Dad won't let me go out this week .....Lo siento, pero mi padre no me deja salir esta semana

Sorry, I'm grounded..Lo siento, estoy castigado/a

Going to a pop concert

The group is giving three concerts in Madrid this autumn ....El grupo va a dar tres conciertos en Madrid este otoño

The first concert will take place in September.....El primer concierto tendrá lugar en setiembre

Where can you buy tickets? ....¿Dónde se puede comprar entradas?

Playing/Watching a game

Shall we play tennis? ....¿Vamos a jugar al tenis?

I'll meet you at the Sports Centre tomorrow evening ....Te veo en el polideportivo mañana por la tarde

I'm not at all fit ....No estoy absolutamente en forma

We would like to go to a football/rugby match ...Queremos ir a un partido de fútbol/rugby

Which team do you support? ....¿De qué equipo eres?

I support Everton...Soy del Everton

At what time does the ice-rink open? ....¿A qué hora se abre la pista de patinaje?

Can you hire skates? ....¿Se puede alquilar patines?

The swimming pool closes at 10.00 pm ....La piscina se cierra a las diez

Would you like to go horse-riding tomorrow afternoon? ....¿Quieres montar a caballo mañana por la tarde?

I'd prefer to go for a walk ....Prefiero dar un paseo

Problems - Great and Small!

At the doctor's

What is the matter? ....¿Qué te/le pasa?

I don't feel well...No me siento bien

I feel ill...Me siento mal/Me siento enfermo/a

My head hurts/aches..Me duele la cabeza

I've hurt my back	Me he lastimado/hecho daño en la espalda
He has trapped his fingers	Se ha pillado los dedos
She has twisted her ankle	Se ha torcido el tobillo
She will have to walk on crutches	Tendrá que andar con muletas
Can you give me something for the pain?	¿Puede darme un analgésico?
I'm allergic to …	Soy alérgico/a a …
I've been stung by a bee/wasp/mosquito	Me ha picado una abeja/una avispa/un mosquito
Here is a prescription for some tablets	Aquí tiene una receta para unos comprimidos
Take one four times a day, after meals	Tome uno cuatro veces al día, después de cada comida
My father has been taken ill	Mi padre se ha puesto enfermo
Will you come and see him, please?	Por favor, venga a verle
Is this the first time that this has happened?	¿Es la primera vez que le ha pasado?
No, it happens quite often	No, me pasa bastante a menudo
I feel dizzy	Me está dando vueltas la cabeza
I've been sick	Acabo de vomitar/He vomitado
Her ankle is swollen	Tiene el tobillo hinchado
The doctor cannot come	El médico no puede venir

At the dentist's

May I have an appointment?	¿Puedo pedir hora para el dentista?
I have toothache	Me duelen las muelas
I've lost a filling	He perdido un empaste
Are you going to give me an injection?	¿Va Vd. a ponerme una inyección?
Pay at reception	Pague en recepción

At the chemist's

Have you got something for a cold?	¿Tiene Vd. algo para el resfriado?
I need some tissues	Quiero unos pañuelos de papel
Can you recommend an insect repellent cream?	¿Puede Vd. recomendarme una crema para ahuyentar los insectos?
I have a temperature	Tengo fiebre
I've got blisters on my right foot	Tengo ampollas en el pie derecho
My brother is suffering from sunburn	Mi hermano tiene una quemadura del sol
Have you got any after-sun cream?	¿Tiene Vd. crema para después del sol?
I would like some plasters/cotton wool	Quiero unas tiritas/algodón
I would like a bottle of cough mixture	Quiero una botella de jarabe para la tos
A large one or a small one?	¿Grande o pequeña?
My sister has stomach-ache	A mi hermana le duele el estómago
She has eaten too many peaches	Ha comido demasiados melocotones
I'm sorry, I don't sell films	Lo siento, no vendo películas/carretes
You'll have to go to the photographer's	Tiene que ir al fotógrafo
The chemist opens at 9.00 am	La farmacia se abre a las nueve

The duty chemist is open on Sunday morning.....La farmacia de guardia esta abierta los domingos por la mañana
I advise you to go to the hospital ....Le aconsejo ir al hospital
It is serious ....Es grave
No, it's not serious ....No, no es grave

Accidents

There has been an accident ....Ha habido un accidente
Where/When did it happen? ....¿Dónde/Cuándo pasó?
What was the weather like? ....¿Qué tiempo hacía?
The boy has been run over ....Han atropellado al niño
He must be taken to hospital................................Es preciso llevarle al hospital
We must phone the police/for an ambulance.......Tenemos que llamar a la policía/una ambulancia
My car is damaged ....Mi coche está estropeado
What is your name and address?..........................Deme sus señas, por favor
Will you write it down for me?............................Quiere Vd. escribírmelo, por favor
He wasn't looking where he was going ....No miraba por dónde iba
Was he going fast?...¿Iba de prisa?
How did the accident happen?.............................¿Cómo ha ocurrido el accidente?
I collided with the car ....Choqué contra el coche
Have you got your driving licence? ....¿Tiene Vd. el permiso de conducir?
Do you want to see my passport?........................¿Quiere ver mi pasaporte?
Have you got your insurance certificate?............¿Tiene Vd. su certificado de seguro?
He was badly hurt ....Estaba gravemente herido
It wasn't his/her right of way ....No tenía prioridad
Where is the first aid kit?....................................¿Dónde está el botiquín?
Don't move her!..¡No la muevan!
Were there any witnesses? ....¿Había testigos?
I saw what happened ....Vi lo que pasó
The accident happened at the crossroads ....El accidente ocurrió en el cruce
It was the lorry driver's fault...............................El camionero tenía toda la culpa
Two people were injured in the accident ....Dos personas fueron heridas en el accidente
It wasn't my fault ....Yo no tenía la culpa
I fell when I was ski-ing.......................................Me caí cuando estaba esquiando
She's fallen in the water.......................................Se cayó al agua
He had left the ball on the stairs..........................Había dejado la pelota en la escalera
My brother has burned himself with some matches .....Mi hermano se ha quemado con unas cerillas
She fell off the horse and broke her arm.............Se cayó del caballo y se rompió el brazo

Minor disasters

I'm sorry I'm late ....Siento mucho llegar tarde
I got lost ....Me perdí
The traffic was heavy ....Había mucho tráfico
I've lost a contact lens/my sunglasses.................Perdí una lentilla/mis gafas de sol

I've broken a plate/glass/cup .... Rompí un plato/un vaso/una taza
I've ripped my pullover .... Me desgarré el jersey
He has lost his calculator .... Ha perdido su calculadora
He dropped a cigarette and burned the carpet...... Dejó caer un cigarillo y quemó la alfombra
He has broken the window .... Ha roto la ventana
I've got oil on my skirt .... Tengo aceite en la falda
Can you clean it for me, please? .... ¿Puede Vd. limpiármelo/limpiármela, por favor?
The sink is blocked .... El fregadero está obstruido
The washing machine is not working .... No funciona la lavadora
My watch is broken.. Mi reloj no funciona
Can you repair it for me? .... ¿Puede Vd. repararmelo/repararmela por favor?
Can you come back for it on Saturday? .... ¿Puede Vd. volver a recogerlo/recogerla el sábado?
That's not possible, I go home tomorrow .... No puedo, vuelvo a casa mañana

At the lost property office

I've lost my passport/camera/mobile .... He perdido mi pasaporte/máquina de fotos/móvil
Where have you looked for it?............................. ¿Por dónde ha buscado?
I've looked in my case/in my room/ everywhere .... He buscado en mi maleta/en mi habitación/ por todas partes
Where did you lose your bag? .... ¿Dónde perdió Vd. su bolsa?
I must have left it on the bus............................... Debo haberlo/haberla dejado en el autobús
When did you lose your umbrella? .... ¿Cuándo perdió Vd. su paraguas?
Yesterday/last week/this morning........................ Ayer/La semana pasada/Esta mañana
My wallet has been stolen.................................... Me han robado la cartera
I put my wallet on the counter .... Puse mi cartera en el mostrador
You'll have to go to the police station................ Hay que ir a la comisaría
What does it look like? .... ¿Cómo es?
It is black and made of leather .... Es negra y de cuero
It has got my name in it .... Tiene mi nombre
It contains 50 euros .... Tiene cincuenta euros

Major disasters

The car crashed into the wall/a tree .... El coche chocó contra el muro/un árbol
There was flooding because of the storms........... Había inundaciones a causa de las tormentas
There's a smell of burning .... Huele a quemado
I can smell smoke .... Huelo humo
There is a fire near the lift.................................. Hay un incendio cerca del ascensor
Ring for the fire brigade....................................... Llame a los bomberos
There has been a bomb scare .... Ha habido una amenaza de bomba
Please leave the building .... Por favor, salgan del edificio
Can you help me, please? .... ¿Puede Vd. ayudarme, por favor?
She has fainted .... Se ha desmayado
He is unconscious .... Está inconsciente

SECTION 2: GENERAL CONVERSATION

Yourself and your family - short answers

What is your name? ....¿Cómo te llamas?
My name is Sue/David..Me llamo Sue/David
How old are you?...¿Cuántos años tienes?
I am 15/16 ....Tengo quince/dieciséis años?
Have you got any brothers or sisters? ....¿Tienes hermanos?
I have a brother and a sister ....Tengo un hermano y una hermana
No, I am an only child..No, soy hijo único/hija única
Is he older than you? ....¿Es mayor que tú?
Is she younger than you?......................................¿Es menor que tú?
My brother is older. My sister is younger ....Mi hermano es mayor. Mi hermana es menor
What does your brother look like?.......................¿Cómo es tu hermano?
My brother is tall..Mi hermano es alto
He has blond hair and blue eyes...........................Tiene el pelo rubio y los ojos azules
What does your sister look like?..........................¿Cómo es tu hermana?
My sister is small ....Mi hermana es pequeña/baja
She has brown hair and brown eyes.....................Tiene el pelo castaño y los ojos marrones
What does your father do? ....¿Qué hace tu padre?
He is a teacher. He works in a secondary school. .....Es profesor. Trabaja en un insti(tuto)
What does your mother do? ....¿Qué hace tu madre?
She is a nurse ....Es enfermera
My parents are separated/divorced......................Mis padres están separados/divorciados
My brother is out of work ....Mi hermano está en paro
My sister is a student..Mi hermana es estudiante
Do you like animals? ....¿Te gustan los animales?
Yes, I like animals..Sí me gustan los animales
Have you got any animals? ....¿Tienes animales?
I have a dog/a cat /a rabbit ....Tengo un perro/un gato/un conejo
Do you prefer dogs or cats? ....¿Prefieres los perros o los gatos?
I prefer cats/dogs..Prefiero los gatos/perros
When is your birthday?..¿Cuando es tu cumpleaños?
My birthday is 26th July ....Mi cumpleaños es el veintiséis de julio
In which year were you born?..............................¿En qué año naciste?
I was born in 1988..Nací en mil novecientos ochenta y ocho
What does your little brother do to annoy you?...¿Qué hace tu hermano para fastidiarte?
He hides my CDs/shoes ....Esconde mis CDs/zapatos
When is your father cross?..................................¿Cuándo está de mal humor tu padre?
When I come home late at night ....Cuando vuelvo tarde a casa por la noche
When I don't do my homework ....Cuando no hago mis deberes

Yourself and your family - longer answers

1. Háblame de ti mismo
Tell me about yourself

Me llamo Chris. Tengo quince años. Mi cumpleaños es el diecinueve de mayo. Nací en mil novecientos ochenta y ocho en Birmingham y ahora vivo en Sutton Coldfield. Soy bastante alto/a. Tengo el pelo rubio y rizado y los ojos azules. Me gusta la música. Mi grupo preferido se llama ...
Soy deportista. Cuando tengo tiempo libre me gusta salir en pandilla con mis amigos/amigas o jugar al tenis. Los fines de semana trabajo en una tienda. Soy dependiente/dependienta

2. Háblame de tu familia
Tell me about your family

Tengo un hermano que se llama Michael. Es mayor que yo. Tiene diecinueve años. Su cumpleaños es el veintiuno de octubre. Trabaja en una oficina en el centro de Birmingham. Es tan alto como yo. Mide un metro sesenta y ocho. Tiene los ojos azules y el pelo castaño. Le interesa el rugby.
No me gusta mucho mi hermano. Es egoísta. Es perezoso y deja sus cosas por todas partes. Nunca hace nada para ayudar en casa. Siempre debo fregar los platos y pasear el perro. Me fastidia.
Mi hermana se llama Claire. Tiene dieciocho años. Su cumpleaños es el veintiuno de junio. Tiene el pelo corto y es pelirrojo. Tiene los ojos verdes. Es más baja que yo. Mide un metro sesenta. Es estudiante. Quiere ser profesora. Le gusta leer e ir al cine. No le gustan los deportes. Me llevo muy bien con mi hermana. Salimos juntos. Me ayuda cuando tengo problemas con mis deberes.
Mi padre es hombre de negocios. Trabaja a Lichfield. Sale de la casa muy temprano por la mañana y vuelve a eso de las siete de la tarde. Los fines de semana le gusta dar paseos y trabajar en el jardín.
Mi madre es enfermera y trabaja a tiempo parcial en el hospital que está a tres kilómetros de nuestra casa. Mi madre es pequeña. Es pelirroja y tiene los ojos marrones. Le gusta ver la televisión y nadar.

3. Háblame de uno de tus amigos/una de tus amigas
Tell me about a friend of yours

Tengo una amiga que vive al lado de nosotros. Se llama Emma. Es muy amable. Tiene quince años como yo. Su cumpleaños es el diecisiete de diciembre. Tiene el pelo castaño y rizado y los ojos marrones también. Mide un metro sesenta y dos. Es más baja que yo. Le gusta tocar la flauta y tocamos juntas en la orquesta del colegio. Le gusta mucho escuchar música, y vamos a la ciudad de vez en cuando durante las vacaciones para comprar CDs. Emma tiene dos hermanos. Son gemelos. Se llaman Andrew y Jonathan. Tienen dieciocho años y a los dos les apasiona el fútbol. El padre de Emma es profesor y su madre es secretaria en el hospital. Emma tiene un perro negro que se llama Bruce y dos conejos que se llaman Peter y Benjamin.

Tengo un amigo que se llama David. Vive muy cerca de nosotros. Es un chico grande con el pelo negro y los ojos marrones. Mide un metro ochenta. Tiene dieciseis años. Su cumpleaños es el ventiséis de julio. Tomamos el autobús para ir al insti(tuto) todos los días y salimos juntos en pandilla con otros amigos los fines de semana. Vamos a un partido de fútbol o vamos a la piscina. A David le gusta jugar al críquet y escuchar música. Le interesa el jazz. Tiene un montón de CDs. Tiene una hermana que se llama Lisa. Lisa tiene doce años y le encantan los animales. Tienen dos gatos y un perro. Su madre es viuda y es farmacéutica.

4. Háblame de tus animales
Tell me about your pets

Me gustan mucho los animales, sobre todo los perros y los gatos. Tengo un perro. Es grande y marrón. Es un collie. Se llama Sandy. Tiene el pelo largo y tengo que cepillarlo bastante a menudo. Lo paseo cada día antes de ir al insti(tuto). Le encanta correr tras una pelota. Tengo dos gatos. Uno se llama Tiger y es negro y blanco. Tiene seis años. Le encanta cazar pájaros en el jardín. La otra es más vieja. Se llama Smudge. Es marrón, negra y blanca. Es la madre de Tiger. Me gustaría comprar unos conejos o cobayas, pero mi madre dice que ya tenemos bastante animales en casa.

Your home - short answers

Where do you live? .... ¿Dónde vives?
I live in Malvern .... Vivo en Malvern
How long have you lived there? .... ¿Desde cuándo vives allí?
I have lived there for thirteen years .... Vivo allí desde hace trece años?
Where did you live before coming to Malvern? .. ¿Dónde vivías antes de venir a Malvern?
I lived in Reading before coming to Malvern ...... Vivía en Reading antes de venir a Malvern
Do you live near school? .... ¿Vives cerca del insti(tuto)?
I live two kilometres from school .... Vivo a dos kilómetros del insti(tuto)
What sort of a house do you live in? .... ¿En qué tipo de casa vives?
I live in a semi-detached house in the suburbs ..... Vivo en una casa adosada en las afueras
I live in a detached house in a small village .... Vivo en una casa en una aldea pequeña
I live in a flat in the centre of town .... Vivo en un piso en el centro de la ciudad
Is your house old or modern? .... ¿Tu casa es vieja o moderna?
My house is (quite) old/modern .... Mi casa es (bastante) vieja/moderna
How many bedrooms are there in your house? .... ¿Cuántos dormitorios hay en tu casa?
There are four .... Hay cuatro
And how many other rooms? .... ¿Y cuántas otras habitaciones?
There are four - the dining room, the kitchen, the living room and the bathroom ..... Hay cuatro - el comedor, la cocina, el salón y el cuarto de baño
Have you a garden? .... ¿Tienes jardín?
Yes, I have a very big garden .... Sí, tengo un jardín muy grande
Have you got your own bedroom? .... ¿Tienes tu propio dormitorio
No, I share with my brother/sister .... No, lo comparto con mi hermano/hermana
Yes, I have my own room. .... Sí, tengo mi propio dormitorio
What furniture do you have in your bedroom? .... ¿Qué muebles tienes en tu habitación?
There is a bed, a wardrobe, a table with a computer, a television and a chair in my bedroom ..... Hay una cama, un armario, una mesa con ordenador, un televisor y una silla en mi habitación

Your home - longer answers

1. Describe tu casa y tu jardín
Describe your house and garden

Mi casa es bastante grande. Es una casa moderna de ladrillo. Nuestra casa está situada en las afueras a cuatro kilómetros del centro de la ciudad. Enfrente de nuestra casa hay un jardin público donde paseamos el perro todos los días. Cuando era pequeño/a, me gustaba jugar en este parque. Tenemos un salón, un comedor y la cocina está en la planta baja. El salón es bastante grande y da al jardín detrás de la casa. En el salón hay *(Insert some details about furniture).* En el primer piso hay tres dormitorios - uno para mis padres, uno para mi hermano y uno para mí. Hay también el cuarto de baño y el aseo. El garaje está al lado de la casa. Tenemos un jardín grande que está detrás de la casa. En nuestro jardín hay árboles, flores, césped y un invernadero. En el verano pasamos mucho tiempo en el jardín cuando hace buen tiempo. A mi padre le gusta trabajar en el jardín. Yo corto el césped.

2. Describe tu habitación
Describe your room

Mi habitación está en el primer piso y da al jardín. Tengo mi propio dormitorio. Es bastante grande. Las paredes de mi dormitorio son azules y las cortinas son amarillas. La alfombra es gris. En mi dormitorio tengo una cama, un armario, una mesa con mi ordenador, una televisión y una silla. Tengo muchos libros, discos compactos. Tengo muchos pósteres bonitos en las paredes. Me gusta escuchar música en mi dormitorio. Cuando mis amigos vienen a verme, siempre vamos a mi dormitorio para charlar, escuchar música o ver la televisión.

Geography - short answers

Where is Malvern?	¿Dónde está Malvern?
Malvern is in Worcestershire, in the centre of England	Malvern está en Worcestershire, en el centro de Inglaterra
How many inhabitants are there?	¿Cuántos habitantes hay?
There are about 36 000 inhabitants	Hay unos treinta y seis mil habitantes
What is there to see in Malvern?	¿Qué hay que ver en Malvern?
You can see the hills, the Priory and a park	Se pueden ver las colinas, el Priorato y un parque
Malvern is a Victorian spa-town	Malvern es un balneario victoriano
What is there to do in Malvern?	¿Qué hay que hacer en Malvern?
One can go to the theatre/cinema/ swimming pool or walk on the hills	Se puede ir al teatro/cine/ a la piscina o dar paseos en las colinas
Is Malvern an industrial town?	¿Es Malvern un pueblo industrial?
Malvern is a tourist town	Malvern es un pueblo turístico
What industries are there in the town?	¿Qué industrias hay en el pueblo?
There are some factories in the town, a sports car factory and some light industry	Hay algunas fábricas en el pueblo, una fábrica donde se construyen coches deportivos, y alguna industria ligera también
What sports facilities are there?	¿Qué hay para hacer deporte?
There is a swimming pool, a tennis club and a football club	Hay una piscina, un club de tenis y un club de fútbol

Are there any interesting places to see around Malvern?................¿Hay algunos sitios de interés alrededor de Malvern?

There are the hills and the city of Worcester.......Hay las colinas y la ciudad de Worcester

Geography - longer answers

1. Describe tu pueblo y los alrededores
Describe your home town and its surroundings

Malvern está situado en Worcestershire en el centro de Inglaterra. Hay treinta y seis mil habitantes, más o menos. Malvern es un balneario victoriano. Es un pueblo turístico. En verano los turistas vienen a dar paseos por las colinas cuando hace buen tiempo. Hay muchos insti(tuto)s y muchas iglesias en Malvern. Hay una piscina, un cine, un teatro y un museo pequeño en el centro del pueblo. Hay algunas fábricas también, incluso una fábrica donde se construyen coches deportivos. No hay muchos grandes almacenes en el centro del pueblo. Para ir a los grandes almacenes hay que ir a Worcester, que está situado a unos quince kilómetros de Malvern.

Birmingham es la segunda ciudad de Inglaterra. Desde el siglo diecinueve es una ciudad industrial muy importante. Birmingham tiene un aeropuerto internacional, muchos teatros, museos de bellas artes y salas de concierto. Birmingham tiene tres universidades y dos equipos de fútbol. Es también una gran ciudad multicultural. Se puede encontrar allí gente que viene de todos los países del mundo. En el centro de la ciudad hay muchos grandes almacenes donde se puede comprar ropa, zapatos, libros o juegos electrónicos. Me gusta mucho dar paseos en el centro de la ciudad con mis amigos los sábados.

2. ¿Qué piensas de tu régión?
What do you think of the area in which you live?

Me gusta mucho el pueblo donde vivo porque hay mucho que hacer: hay cines y muchos grandes almacenes en el centro de la ciudad. Se puede ir a ver películas buenas, ir a bailar en las discotecas o ir a curiosear por las tiendas con mis amigos. Hay un autobús cada diez minutos. Puedo salir sin pedir a mis padres que me lleven en coche. Los fines de semana se puede hacer deporte porque hay una piscina, una pista de patinaje y un polideportivo muy grande.

No me gusta el pueblo donde vivo porque no hay nada que hacer para los jóvenes. No hay muchas tiendas. El cine es demasiado pequeño y no ponen nunca las películas que queremos ver. No hay ni piscina ni polideportivo. Sólo hay dos autobuses por la mañana y dos por la tarde. Si tengo ganas de salir tengo que ir a pie o en bici, o pedir a mis padres que me lleven en coche. No es muy práctico. Me gusta ver grandes almacenes, polideportivos y buenas cafeterías donde puedo ir con los amigos.

3. ¿Vivir en la ciudad o en el campo? ¿Cuál prefiere(s)? ¿Por qué?
Living in the town or the country - Which do you prefer, and why?

Me gusta más vivir en la ciudad. Siempre hay diversiones. Se puede salir fácilmente por la tarde. *(Insert name of your town)* es un centro cultural; hay polideportivos para hacer los deportes. Hay un centro comercial con muchos grandes almacenes y restaurantes. Se encuentra lejos del tráfico en la zona peatonal. Hay autobuses y trenes si se quiere viajar. Es muy agradable vivir en la ciudad.
Me gusta más vivir en el campo. La vida es más tranquila y el aire está menos contaminado. Se puede dar paseos largos a lo largo del río. Se puede ir a pescar. En una aldea todo el mundo se conoce. Creo

que se puede sentirse solo en una gran ciudad. El tráfico no es un problema. Seguro que hay inconvenientes. Puede ser difícil ir a la ciudad si no hay coche, y no hay ni cine ni club de jóvenes en un pueblo.

Daily routine - short answers

What time do you get up?......¿A qué hora te levantas?
I get up at 7.00......Me levanto a las siete
What time do you have breakfast?......¿A qué hora tomas el desayuno?
I have breakfast at 8.15......Tomo el desayuno a las ocho y cuarto
What do you usually have for breakfast?......¿Qué tomas normalmente para el desayuno?
I usually have toast and cereal for breakfast......Normalmente tomo pan tostado y cereales
I don't have breakfast......No tomo desayuno

What time do you leave home?......¿A qué hora sales de casa?
I leave home at 8.30......Salgo de casa a las ocho y media
What time do you arrive at school?......¿A qué hora llegas al insti(tuto)?
I arrive at school at 8.45......Llego a las nueve menos cuarto
How do you come to school?......¿Cómo vienes al insti(tuto)?
I come to school by bus/car/bike......Vengo en autobús/coche/bicicleta
I walk to school......Vengo al insti(tuto) a pie

When do lessons start?......¿A qué hora empiezan las clases?
Lessons start at 9.00......Las clases empiezan a las nueve
How long are the lessons in your school?......¿Cuánto tiempo duran las clases en tu insti(tuto)?
They last one hour five minutes......Duran una hora y cinco minutos
What do you do during break?......¿Qué haces durante el recreo?
I talk to my friends during break......Durante el recreo charlo con mis amigos
When is your lunch time?......¿A qué hora comes el almuerzo?
Lunch time is at 12.30......Como el almuerzo a las doce y media
Do you eat in the canteen at lunch time?......¿Comes en el comedor del colegio a mediodía?
Yes, I eat in the canteen at lunch time......Sí, como en el comedor del colegio a mediodía
What do you eat at lunch time?......¿Qué comes a mediodía?
I have sandwiches at lunch time......Como bocadillos a mediodía
When does school end?......¿A qué hora terminan las clases?
School ends at 3.40......Terminan a las cuatro menos veinte
What time do you get home?......¿A qué hora llegas otra vez a casa?
I get home at 4.10......Llego a casa a las cuatro y diez

What time do you have your evening meal?......¿A qué hora cenas/tomas la cena?
I have my evening meal at six o' clock......Ceno/Tomo la cena a las seis
What do you eat in the evening?......¿Qué comes por la noche?
In the evening I have soup, meat, vegetables and ice cream......Por la noche como sopa, carne, legumbres y helado
What is your favourite food?......¿Cuál es tu comida preferida?
My favourite food is ......Mi comida preferida es ...

Is there anything you don't like?..........................¿Hay algo que no te gusta?
I don't like carrots..No me gustan las zanahorias

What do you do in the evening? ....¿Qué haces por la tarde?
I do my homework and listen to music ....Hago mis deberes y escucho música
in the evening por las tardes
Do you help your parents prepare the meal?........¿Ayudas a tus padres a preparar la comida?
No, but I have to do the washing up ....No, pero tengo que fregar los platos
Do you watch TV in the evening? ....¿Ves la televisión por la tarde?
Yes, sometimes ....Sí, a veces
What time do you go to bed? ....¿A qué hora te acuestas?
I go to bed at 10:30 ....Me acuesto a las diez y media
What do you do to help in the house?.................¿Qué haces para ayudar en casa?
I have to tidy my room ....Tengo que arreglar mi dormitorio

Saturday jobs

Do you have a Saturday job? ....¿Trabajas los sábados?
Yes, I work on Saturday morning ....Sí, trabajo los sábados por la mañana
Where do you work?..¿Dónde trabajas?
I work in a shop...Trabajo en una tienda
I work in a restaurant ....Trabajo en un restaurante
What is your job?..¿Qué haces?
I am a sales assistant ....Soy dependiente/dependienta
I do babysitting..Hago de canguro
I am saving up for ... .Estoy ahorrando para ...
I prefer to earn money ....Prefiero ganar dinero
I would like to buy a computer ....Me gusaría comprar un ordenador
No, I can't work Saturdays, I am in school..........No, no puedo trabajar los sábados, voy al insti(tuto)

Who does what?

I like walking the dog when it is fine..................Me gusta pasear el perro cuando hace buen tiempo
I hate washing up. It's a boring job......................Odio fregar los platos. Es una tarea muy aburrida
I prefer ironing. I listen to music while I work ....Prefiero planchar la ropa. Escucho música mientras trabajo
My brother never washes up. It's not fair!...........Mi hermano nunca friega los platos. ¡No es justo!
My sister never walks the dog.............................Mi hermana nunca pasea el perro
when it's raining cuando está lloviendo
I always have to wash the car and.......................Siempre tengo que lavar el coche
mow the lawn y cortar el césped

Daily routine - past tense

What did you watch on TV last night? ....¿Qué viste en la televisión anoche?
I watched some cartoons......................................Vi unos dibujos animados
What did you do to help your mother? ....¿Qué hiciste para ayudar a tu madre?
I walked the dog and went shopping ....Paseé el perro y fui de compras
What did you have for breakfast this morning?...¿Qué tomaste de desayuno esta mañana?
I had toast and tea ....Tomé pan tostado y té
How did you come to school this morning? ....¿Cómo viniste al insti(tuto) esta mañana?
I walked ....Vine a pie

Daily routine - future tense

What are you going to do this evening? ....¿Qué vas a hacer esta tarde?
I'll do my homework and watch TV....................Haré mis deberes y veré la televisión
What are you going to watch on TV this evening?....¿Qué vas a ver en la tele esta tarde?
I am going to watch *The Bill*...............................Voy a ver *The Bill*
What will you have for lunch?.............................¿Qué vas a tomar para el almuerzo?
I will have sandwiches for lunch ....Voy a tomar bocadillos para el almuerzo
What will you have this evening?........................¿Qué vas a tomar esta tarde?
We will have chicken, chips and peas ....Vamos a tomar pollo, patatas fritas y guisantes
What will you be doing at the weekend?.............¿Qué harás el fin de semana?
I will go out (in a group) with my friends...........Saldré (en pandilla) con mis amigos

Daily routine - longer answers

1. Describe un día típico durante la semana
Describe a typical weekday

Me levanto a las siete y media, me ducho, luego me visto, me peino y bajo para tomar el desayuno. Salgo de casa y cojo el autobús para venir al insti(tuto). Llego a las nueve menos diez. Las clases empiezan a las nueve. Tenemos tres clases por la mañana, dos antes del recreo y una después. A mediodía como bocadillos. Por la tarde tenemos tres clases y el insti(tuto) termina a las cuatro menos cuarto. Vuelvo a casa, veo la televisión, hago mis deberes y cenamos a las seis. De vez en cuando salgo (en pandilla) con mis amigos. Me acuesto a las once.

2. ¿Qué hiciste antes de venir al insti(tuto) esta mañana?
What did you do before coming to school this morning?

Me desperté a las siete y cuarto. Me levanté a las siete y media y me duché. Luego me limpié los dientes, me peiné, me vestí y bajé a la cocina para tomar el desayuno. Mis padres tomaron el desayuno también. Mi padre salió de casa a las ocho. Comí pan tostado y bebí una taza de café. Puse mis libros y mis carpetas en mi mochila, y salí de la casa a las ocho y diez. Fui a pie a la parada de autobús. El autobús llegó a las nueve menos veinticinco. Llegué al insti(tuto) a las nueve menos diez.

3. Describe un fin de semana típico
Describe a typical weekend

Los sábados por la mañana me levanto a las siete y media como siempre porque trabajo en un supermercado en la caja, y tengo que estar allí para las ocho y media. Trabajo toda la mañana y termino a la una. Vuelvo a casa, como un bocadillo y luego me pongo mis vaqueros para salir con mis amigos. De vez en cuando vamos a un partido o vamos a la ciudad para curiosear. Por la tarde vamos al cine o a una fiesta. Volvemos tarde. ¡El domingo duermo tarde! Me levanto a eso de mediodía, veo la televisión o una película en vídeo, y por la tarde hago mis deberes.

Soy interno/a, así es que normalmente estoy en el insti(tuto) los fines de semana. Los sábados por la mañana me levanto a las siete y media como siempre, me lavo, me visto y me peino, luego voy a tomar el desayuno. Por la mañana hay clases y por la tarde hacemos deporte. Por la tarde vemos la televisión o escuchamos música. A veces tenemos permiso para ir a la ciudad o volvemos a casa para pasar el fin de semana.
Los domingos nos levantamos más tarde. Vamos a la iglesia, luego comemos. Por la tarde podemos ir a la ciudad. A menudo veo amigos/amigas de otro internado. Más tarde hacemos deporte, leemos, jugamos a las cartas. Está bastante bien, pero no es siempre divertido.

School - short answers

How many pupils are there in your school?	¿Cuántos alumnos/alumnas hay en tu insti(tuto)?
There are 1400 pupils in the school	Hay mil cuatrocientos alumnos/as en el insti(tuto)
How many pupils are there in your class?	¿Cuántos alumnos/alumnas hay en tu clase?
There are 27 pupils in my class	Hay veintisiete alumnos/alumnas en mi clase
Do you wear school uniform?	¿Llevas uniforme (escolar)?
Do you like your uniform?	¿Te gusta tu uniforme?
No, I do not like/Yes, I do like my school uniform	No, no me gusta/Sí, me gusta mi uniforme
Which subjects do you do?	¿Qué asignaturas estudias?
I do English, Maths, French, Spanish, Science, Art, IT, History, Geography and Technology	Estudio inglés, matemáticas, francés, español, ciencias, dibujo, informática, historia, geografía y tecnología
Which is your favourite subject?	¿Cuál es tu asignatura preferida?
My favourite subject is Spanish	Mi asignatura preferida es el español
Why?	¿Por qué?
I get good marks	Saco buenas notas
because it's interesting	porque es interesante
because the teacher is nice	porque el profesor/la profesora es simpático/a
Which subject don't you like?	¿Qué asignatura no te gusta?
I don't like Chemistry	No me gusta la química
Which subjects are you good at?	¿Qué asignaturas se te dan bien?
I am good at English	Se me da bien el inglés
Which is your worst subject?	¿Qué asignaturas se te dan mal?
I'm very bad at Physics	Se me da muy mal la física
Are you in a school team?	¿Juegas en algún equipo en el insti(tuto)?
I play in the school hockey/rugby team	Juego en el equipo de hockey/rugby

Which sport do you prefer?	¿Cuál es tu deporte preferido?
I prefer tennis	Prefiero el tenis
Are you in the orchestra/choir/band?	¿Eres miembro de la orquesta/del coro/de la banda?
I sing in the choir	Canto en el coro
What do you like about school life?	¿Qué te gusta de la vida en el insti(tuto)?
I like being with my friends and I like sport	Me gusta estar con mis amigos y me gustan los deportes
What do you dislike about school life?	¿Qué no te gusta de la vida en el insti(tuto)?
I don't like some lessons	Hay algunas clases que no me gustan
I don't like the uniform	No me gusta el uniforme
What irritates you in school?	¿Qué te fastidia en el insti(tuto)?
School uniform irritates me	El uniforme escolar me fastidia
What bores you in school?	¿Qué te aburre en el insti(tuto)?
Some of the school rules bore me	Algunas de las reglas del insti(tuto) me aburren

School - past tense

Have you ever been on an exchange?	¿Has hecho un intercambio escolar?
I went on an exchange to Spain last year	Hice un intercambio en España el año pasado
I went to France two years ago	Fui a Francia hace dos años
Where did you go?	¿Adónde fuiste?
I went to Pontevedra/Nantes	Fui a Pontevedra/Nantes
How long were you in Spain/France?	¿Cuánto tiempo te quedaste en España/Francia?
We spent ten days there	Pasamos diez días allí
What did you do there?	¿Qué hiciste allí?
We visited the city	Visitamos la ciudad
We went on some trips	Hicimos algunas excursiones
We went to school with our friends	Fuimos al insti(tuto) con nuestros amigos
What did you think of the exchange?	¿Qué te pareció el intercambio?
I had a good time	Lo pasé bomba
I would like to go back there	Me gustaría volver allí
My Spanish/French family was very nice	Mi familia española/francesa era muy simpática
I liked (did not like) Spanish/French food	(No) Me gustaba la comida española/francesa
The visit was too long	La visita fue demasiado larga
I missed my family	Echaba de menos a mi familia
What did you do at school yesterday?	¿Qué hiciste en el insti(tuto) ayer?
I did history, geography and maths	Estudié historia, geografía y matemáticas
What time did you get to school yesterday?	¿A qué hora llegaste al insti(tuto) ayer?
I was late	Llegué tarde

School and future plans

What lessons have you got tomorrow?	¿Qué clases tienes mañana?
I shall have French, English and biology	Tendré francés, inglés y biología
What are you doing after school tomorrow?	¿Qué harás mañana después del colegio?
I've got a rehearsal	Tendré un ensayo

What are you going to do after the exams?..........¿Qué vas a hacer después de los exámenes?
I shall work for a few weeks, then go on holiday ....Voy a trabajar durante unas semanas, luego iré de vacaciones
What will you be doing next year? ....¿Qué vas a hacer el año que viene?
Will you be coming back to school?....................¿Volverás al insti(tuto)?
I think I shall be coming back ....Creo que volveré
That will depend on my exam results ....Depende de los resultados de mis exámenes
No, I'm leaving school..No, voy a dejar el insti(tuto)
If I pass my exams, I shall do A Levels ....Si apruebo los exámenes, voy a estudiar para los A Levels/el bachillerato
Where will you be going? ....¿Adónde irás?
I shall go to the 6th form college in Worcester....Iré al insti(tuto)/colegio de tercero de BUP y COU en Worcester
Will you be taking A levels?...............................¿Vas a hacer el bachillerato?
Yes, I am going to do A levels............................Sí, voy a hacer el bachillerato
What subjects are you planning to do? ....¿Qué asugnaturas vas a hacer?
I would like to do Spanish, Maths and Music......Me gustaría estudiar español, matemáticas y música
No, I prefer to do AVCE.....................................No, prefiero hacer una formación profesional
What will you do when you have left school?.....¿Qué vas a hacer después de dejar el insti(tuto)?
Will you be going to university?..........................¿Vas a ir a la universidad?
I hope to go to university ....Espero ir a la universidad
Would you like to do an apprenticeship?............¿Te gustaría estar de aprendiz/aprendiza?
Yes, I am going to do an apprenticeship.............Sí, voy a estar de aprendiz/aprendiza
I shall be an apprentice in an engineering works. .....Seré aprendiz(a) en un taller de ingeniería
Will you start work/a job? ....¿Vas a empezar a trabajar?
Yes, I am going to work in my father's office .....Sí, voy a trabajar en la oficina de mi padre
What sort of job would you like to get?..............¿Qué tipo de trabajo te gustaría obtener?
I would like to be a primary school teacher because I'd like to work with children ....Me gustaría ser maestro/maestra de escuela porque me gustaría trabajar con niños
I'd like to be a pilot because I'd like to travel......Me gustaría ser piloto porque me gustaría viajar
I'd like to be a hairdresser..................................Me gustaría ser peluquero/peluquera

School - longer answers

1. Háblame de tu insti(tuto) y del uniforme escolar
Tell me about your school and the uniform

Mi insti(tuto) está situado a tres kilómetros del centro de la ciudad. Es un edifico grande de ladrillo rojo que data de los años cincuenta. Hay muchas aulas, muchos laboratorios y talleres. Hay campos de fútbol, campos de rugby, campos de hockey y un gran gimnasio, pero desafortunadamente no hay piscina. Hay mil quinientos alumnos en el insti, más o menos, y ochenta profesores.
Tenemos que llevar uniforme escolar. Las chicas llevan una falda azul marino y una blusa blanca, un jersey azul marino, una corbata azul marino y amarilla y zapatos negros. Los chicos llevan un pantalón gris con una corbata azul marino y amarilla, una camisa blanca y un jersey azul marino. Hay que decir que no me gusta el uniforme, porque los colores son tristes, pero es práctico.

2. Háblame de tu horario
Tell me about your timetable

Tengo treinta clases cada semana. Hay seis clases cada día - dos antes del recreo, una después, y tres por la tarde. Las clases empiezan a las nueve y el colegio termina a las cuatro. Estudio inglés, matemáticas, español, francés, ciencias, informática, geografía y tecnología.

Me gustan mucho las ciencias y la informática, y se me da bien el inglés. Soy regular en matemáticas y francés, y encuentro bastante difícil el español. Me interesa la tecnología, pero se me da muy mal la geografía.

Me gusta hacer gimnasia y jugar al tenis, pero no me gusta jugar al hockey en el invierno cuando llueve y cuando hace frío.

3. Dime lo que pretendes hacer en el futuro
Tell me what you plan to do in the future

El año que viene quiero empezar a estudiar el bachillerato. Quiero estudiar ciencias naturales porque creo que la biología es muy interesante. Creo que podría ir a la universidad y después de terminar mis estudios quiero hacer investigaciones. Las investigaciones científicas son muy importantes para la medicina y para el progreso en general.

Free time and hobbies - short answers

What do you do when you have some free time? .....¿Qué haces cuando tienes tiempo libre?
I go out (in a group) with my friends..................Salgo (en pandilla) con mis amigos
What do you do at weekends? ....¿Qué haces los fines de semana?
I play football/watch TV.....................................Juego al fútbol/Veo la televisión
Where do you go with your friends at weekends? ....¿A dónde vas con los amigos los fines de semana?
I go to a cinema/disco/the youth club ....Voy al cine/a la discoteca/al club de jóvenes
Do you like sport?..¿Te gustan los deportes?
Yes, I like sport very much.................................Sí, me gustan mucho los deportes
Which is your favourite sport? ....¿Cuál es tu deporte preferido?
I like tennis/rugby ....Me gusta el tenis/el rugby
Where/When do you play? ....¿Dónde/Cuándo juegas?
I play on Saturday afternoon...............................Juego los sábados por la tarde
Are you a member of a club?..............................¿Eres miembro/miembra de un club?
Yes, I belong to a tennis club..............................Sí, soy miembro/miembra de un club de tenis
Are you interested in music? ....¿Te interesa la música?
Yes, music is very important to me ....Sí, la música es muy importante para mí
What type of music do you like? ....¿Qué tipo de música te gusta?
I prefer classical music ....Prefiero la música clásica
Have you got a favourite group/singer?..............¿Tienes un grupo/cantante preferido?
No, I haven't got a favourite group/singer...........No, no tengo grupo/cantante preferido
Do you play an instrument?................................¿Tocas algún instrumento?
Yes, I play the violin/the clarinet........................Sí, toco el violín/el clarinete
How long have you been playing the clarinet?....¿Desde hace cuánto tiempo tocas el clarinete?
I have been playing the clarinet for four years.....Toco el clarinete desde hace cuatro años

Do you watch much TV at weekends?	¿Ves mucho la televisión los fines de semana?
It depends	Depende
What sort of programme do you like?	¿Qué tipo de programa te gusta?
I like documentaries/cartoons	Me gustan los documentales/los dibujos animados
What sort of programme do you not like?	¿Qué tipo de programa no te gusta?
I don't like the news	No me gusta el telediario
No, I don't watch TV very often	No, no veo la televisión muy a menudo
Do you like going to the cinema?	¿Te gusta ir al cine?
Yes, I like going to the cinema sometimes	Sí, me gusta ir al cine de vez en cuando
How often do you go to the cinema?	¿Con qué frecuencia vas al cine?
Two or three times a year	Dos o tres veces al año
Which type of film do you like best?	¿Qué tipo de película te gusta más?
I like science fiction	Me gusta la ciencia ficción
Do you like reading?	¿Te gusta leer?
Yes, I like reading	Sí, me gusta leer
What type of books do you like?	¿Qué tipo de libros te gustan?
I like detective stories	Me gustan las novelas policíacas
Do you collect CDs/stickers?	¿Coleccionas discos compactos/pegatinas?
Yes, I collect CDs	Sí, colecciono discos compactos
Have you got a computer?	¿Tienes ordenador?
Yes, I have a computer at home	Sí, tengo un ordenador en casa
Do you play computer games?	¿Juegas con juegos electrónicos?
Yes, I have a lot of computer games	Sí, tengo muchos juegos electrónicos
Are you interested in fashion?	¿Te interesa la moda?
Yes, I am very interested in fashion	Sí, me interesa mucho la moda
Do you like window shopping?	¿Te gusta curiosear por las tiendas?
Yes, I like window shopping with my friends	Sí, me gusta curiosear con mis amigos
Which shops do you like looking round?	¿En qué tiendas te gusta curiosear?
I like looking around bookshops/record shops	Me gusta curiosear por las librerías/tiendas de discos
Are you going out this evening?	¿Sales esta tarde?
No, my mother won't let me go out in the week	No, mi madre no me permite salir durante la semana

Free time and hobbies - past tense

What did you do last Saturday?	¿Qué hiciste el sábado pasado?
I went to the cinema	Fui al cine
What did you think of the film?	¿Qué te pareció la película?
I thought it was good	Me pareció buena
The actors were superb	Los actores eran magníficos
The film was too long	La película era demasiado larga
The actors were poor	Los actores eran bastante malos
Where did you see it?	¿Dónde la viste?
I went to a cinema in Birmingham	Fui a un cine en Birmingham

When did you see it?..¿Cuándo la viste?
I saw it a month ago..La vi hace un mes
Is it out on video? ....¿Ya está en vídeo?
What did you do last night?................................¿Qué hiciste anoche?
I stayed at home..Me quedé en casa
What did you see on TV last night?.....................¿Qué viste en la televisión anoche?
I did not watch TV..No vi la televisión
What did you buy last Saturday?.........................¿Qué compraste el sábado pasado?
I bought a birthday present for my father............Compré un regalo para el cumpleaños de mi padre

Free time and hobbies - future tense

What are you going to do at the weekend?..........¿Qué vas a hacer el fin de semana que viene?
I am going to see my cousins in Madrid..............Voy a ver a mis primos en Madrid
I am going to play rugby.....................................Voy a jugar al rugby
I shall be working at the supermarket.................Voy a trabajar en el supermercado

Free time and hobbies - longer answers

1. **Dime qué tipo de película prefieres**
   Tell me what sort of film you like

Me gustan las películas de miedo porque me gusta ver los efectos especiales y los monstruos que se construyen. Si estoy con amigos, encuentro divertido mirarlos durante estas películas para ver si tienen miedo.
Me gusta también ver las películas de ciencia-ficción, porque me gustan mucho los cohetes y los viajes en el espacio.

2. **Dime qué tipo de programa te gusta ver en la televisión y por qué te gusta**
   Tell me what type of programme you like watching on television and say why you like it

Me gusta ver los programas de historia natural, porque encuentro emocionantes los animales salvajes y los pájaros – sobre todo las especies en peligro de extinción. Me gusta mucho verlos en su hábitat, pero no me gusta verlos en los zoos. Me gusta ver las flores exóticas. Los colores son tan hermosos. Le televisión nos permite ver todas estas cosas maravillosas.

3. **Háblame de lo que haces depués del colegio**
   Tell me what you do after school

Soy deportista y los domingos por la tarde juego en un equipo de fútbol/hockey. Los martes canto en el coro y los jueves voy a la piscina con algunos amigos/algunas amigas.
Trabajo los sábados. Soy dependiente/dependienta en unos grandes almacenes en el centro de la ciudad. Los sábados paso la tarde con unos amigos. Vamos al cine o a una discoteca. Si no tenemos bastante dinero para salir pasamos la tarde escuchando música o viendo la televisión.

4. Dime qué deporte prefieres y dame tus razones
Tell me which sport you prefer and give your reasons

Me gusta mucho jugar al tenis. Es un juego emocionante. Es muy importante para la salud mantenerse en forma. Soy miembro/miembra de un club, y veo a unos amigos/unas amigas cada vez que voy allí. Los fines de semana voy a menudo a otros clubs para ver partidos. Llego a conocer a mucha gente. Me gusta ver el tenis en la televisión, porque se puede aprender muchas cosas viendo jugar a los profesionales.

5. ¿Qué piensas de la publicidad en la televisión?
What do you think of television adverts?

La publicidad en la televisión me fastidia. A veces la encuentro divertida, pero normalmente la encuentro estúpida. Es tiempo perdido. Hay demasiada publicidad que interrumpe los programas y no se puede ver una película sin interrupción. Odio la publicidad de coches. ¡A menudo voy a hacerme una taza de café!

6. ¿Qué haces para mantenerte en forma?
What do you do to get fit?

Creo que los deportes son muy importantes para la salud. Para mantenerse en forma, es preciso hacerse deporte. Se puede escoger un deporte individual, por ejemplo la natación o el footing. Puedes hacerte miembro/miembra de un club de deportes, si quieres hacer deportes con otra gente. Los deportes de equipo son muy buenos para la salud y también para pasarlo bomba con los amigos.
No fumo y presto atención a lo que como. Como legumbres, pastas, arroz, fruta, bebo zumo de fruta. Escojo pollo y no como ni salchichas, ni hamburguesas, ni patatas fritas. No como fritas, no como mucho queso, no como pasteles. ¡No es siempre muy agradable, porque me gustan mucho el chocolate y el queso!

Shopping - short answers

Do you like going shopping? ....¿Te gusta ir de compras?
Yes, I like/No, I don't like shopping....................Sí me gusta/No, no me gusta ir de compras
I prefer buying clothes ....Prefiero comprar ropa
I don't like going to the supermarket ....No me gusta ir al supermercado
When do you go shopping?.................................¿Cuándo vas de compras?
I go shopping on Saturday afternoon ....Voy de compras los sábados por la tarde
Who do you go shopping with? ....¿Con quién vas de compras?
I like going with my friends ....Me gusta ir con mis amigos
They tell me what they think...............................Me dicen lo que piensan
I don't like going with my mother ....No me gusta ir con mi madre
I don't like the clothes she likes..........................No me gusta la ropa que a ella le gusta
I like buying clothes on my own ....Me gusta comprar ropa solo/sola
Do you like buying presents?..............................¿Te gusta comprar regalos?
I like buying presents for people my own age......Me gusta comprar regalos para la gente de mi edad
I never know what to give my grandparents ....Nunca sé qué regalar a mis abuelos

Shopping - longer answers

1. ¿Qué hiciste el sábado pasado?
What did you do last Saturday?

El sábado pasado fui al centro de la cuidad. Estaba con mis amigos/amigas. Decidimos ir a comprar ropa. Compré un traje de baño y unas sandalias. Mi amigo/amiga Chris quería comprar unos vaqueros. ¡Tuvo bastante problemas! El color no era bueno. Quería comprar esta marca y no aquella. Finalmente encontró lo que quería y fuimos a comer. *(Insert what you ate and drank and where you went for the meal).* Volvimos a casa a las tres y media.

2. ¿Qué ropa comprarías si pudieras eligir?
What clothes would you buy if you had the choice?

Compraría ropa para todas las ocasiones - vestidos, faldas, blusas, jerseys y muchos zapatos. Me gusta llevar vaqueros y un jersey cuando estoy en casa, pero por la tarde me gusta llevar un vestido bonito o una falda cuando salgo con mis amigos/amigas. No me gusta llevar vestidos ni faldas a menudo. Mi color preferido es el azul.

Holidays - short answers

Where are you going on holiday? ....¿Adónde vas de vacaciones?
I'm going to the seaside to visit my grandparents ....Voy a orillas del mar para visitar a mis abuelos
Do you spend your holidays in England? ....¿Pasas las vacaciones en Inglaterra?
Yes, I spend a fortnight in Devon ....Sí, paso quince días en Devon
No, I go to Spain/Greece......................................No, voy a España/Grecia
Do you go with your family or with friends?.......¿Vas con la familia o con amigos?
I usually go with my family ....Normalmente voy con mi familia
This year I am going with my friends ....Este año voy con mis amigos
Do you go camping? ....¿Haces camping?
Sometimes we go camping in Spain ....A veces hacemos camping en España
What do you like doing on holiday? ....¿Qué te gusta hacer de vacaciones?
I like walking and swimming...............................Me gusta dar paseos y nadar
What sort of souvenirs do you buy? ....¿Qué tipo de recuerdos compras?
I buy postcards, pottery, a T-shirt ....Compro tarjetas postales, cerámica, una camiseta

Holidays - past tense

Where did you go on holiday last summer? ....¿Adónde fuiste de vacaciones el verano pasado?
Last year we went to Greece ....El año pasado fuimos a Grecia
How did you get there?..¿Cómo llegaste hasta allí?
We flew..Volamos
How long did you stay? ....¿Cuánto tiempo te quedaste?
We stayed a fortnight/three weeks ....Nos quedamos quince días/tres semanas
What was the weather like? ....¿Qué tiempo hacía?
It was hot and sunny ....Hacía calor y hacía sol
Did you go swimming/spend time on the beach? .....¿Nadaste/Pasaste tiempo en la playa?
Yes, we went to the beach every day ....Sí, fuimos a la playa todos los días
Did you visit any interesting places? ....¿Visitaste algunos sitios de interés?

Yes, we went to Athens. ....Sí, fuimos a Atenas
It was very interesting..Fue muy interesante
What did you do in the evening? ....¿Qué hiciste por la tarde?
In the evening we went to a restaurant.................Por la tarde fuimos a un restaurante
We walked around the town ....Dimos un paseo por la ciudad
We went to a café/night club ....Fuimos a un café/una sala de fiestas
Would you like to go there again? ....¿Te gustaría volver allí otra vez?
Yes, I would very much like to go there again.....Sí, me gustaría volver allí otra vez

Holidays - future tense

Are you going away at Easter?.............................¿Vas a marchar para Semana Santa?
No, I shall spend the Easter holidays at home .....No, voy a pasar las vacaciones de Pascua en casa
Where do you plan to go this summer? ....¿Adónde piensas ir este verano?
I don't know...No sé
We have not yet decided.....................................No hemos decidido todavía
We are going to the USA....................................Vamos a ir a los Estados Unidos
Will you be going with friends/your family?.......¿Irás con amigos/tu familia?
I shall go there with my parents..........................Iré allí con mis padres
Will you go camping?..¿Harás camping?
Will you be staying in a hotel?............................¿Te alojarás en un hotel?
Will you rent a flat? ....¿Alquilarás un piso?
We shall stay with my uncle and aunt.................Nos alojaremos con mis tíos
How will you get there?.......................................¿Cómo llegarás allí?
We shall fly to New York ....Volaremos hasta Nueva York
How long will you be staying? ....¿Para cuánto tiempo te quedarás?
We are planning to stay a month.........................Tenemos pensado quedarnos un mes
What are you going to do there?..........................¿Qué vas a hacer allí?
We hope to be able to visit Washington ....Esperamos poder visitar Washington

Holidays - longer answers

1 Dime lo que hiciste durante las vacaciones del verano pasado
Tell me what you did during last summer holidays

El año pasado trabajé un mes en la oficina de mi padre. Quería ganar dinero para mis vacaciones en Escocia. Trabajé desde el dieciocho de julio hasta el dieciséis de agosto. Empezaba a trabajar a las nueve y terminaba a las cinco y media. Me ocupaba del correo, contestaba el teléfono y archivaba documentos.
El diecisiete de agosto fui con mis amigos a Escocia. Hicimos camping. Pasamos quince días cerca de Callander. Hacía buen tiempo y pudimos visitar la ciudad y dar paseos largos por la montaña. Me gusta mucho dar paseos por la montaña cuando hace buen tiempo. Éramos seis personas, tres chicas y tres chicos. Lo pasamos bomba. Quiero volver allí un día de estos.

El año pasado fui con mi familia a pasar tres semanas en Italia. Cogimos el avión para ir a Roma y alquilamos un coche para hacer excursiones. Pasamos unos días en Roma y fuimos a Venecia y a

Florencia. Visitamos museos, iglesias y tiendas bonitas. Luego pasamos diez días a orillas del mar. Hacía un tiempo espléndido. Me gusta mucho la comida italiana. Aprendí unas palabras en italiano.

2 ¿Cómo vas a pasar las vacaciones de Pascua/Semana Santa?
How will you be spending the Easter holidays?

Tendremos dos semanas de vacaciones de Pascua. Me quedaré en casa. Mi amigo español/amiga española va a pasar una semana con nosotros. Si hace buen tiempo, haremos excursiones en coche y en bici para ver la región. Es deportista. Iremos a la piscina y a la pista de patinaje. La segunda semana iremos a ver a mi primo que vive en Gales. Vive en Cardiff y me gusta ir a Cardiff. Es una gran ciudad interesante donde siempre hay mucho que hacer.

3. ¿Qué harías si te tocase El Gordo?
What would you do if you won the lottery?

Si me tocase El Gordo, compraría mucha ropa *(Give details)*, iría a Australia para ver a mis primos *(Say where they live, etc)*, visitaría *Disneylandia* en los Estados Unidos *(Say what you would do)*.

Special occasions - short answers

When is your birthday?..¿Cuándo es tu cumpleaños?
My birthday is on 14th December ....Mi cumpleaños es el catorce de diciembre
What do you do on your birthday? ....¿Qué haces para celebrar tu cumpleaños?
My family give me presents and cards.................Mi familia me da regalos y cartas
What do you do at Christmas?.............................¿Qué haces para celebrar las Navidades?
We give each other presents, we go to church.....Nos damos regalos, vamos a la iglesia
What other festivals do you celebrate?................¿Qué otras fiestas celebras?
We celebrate Passover/Eid/Divali ....Celebramos la Pascua judía/Eid/Divali
When is Passover/Eid/Divali? ....¿Cuándo es la Pascua judía/Eid/Divali?
Do you give presents?...¿Os dais regalos?
Do you spend the day with your family? ....¿Pasas el día con tu familia?
Yes, family life is very important ....Sí, la vida de familia es muy importante

Special occasions - past tense

What did you have for Christmas? ....¿Qué regalos recibiste por Navidades?
My grandparents gave me some clothes ....Mis abuelos me dieron ropa
My parents gave me a mountain bike/ a computer ....Mis padres me dieron una bici de montaña/ un ordenador
What did you give your parents for Christmas? ..¿Qué regalos diste a tus padres?
I gave my father a bottle of wine ....Di una botella de vino a mi padre
I gave my mother a book ....Di un libro a mi madre
What did you give your brother/sister?................¿Qué regalos diste a tu hermano/hermana?
I gave my brother a CD.......................................Di un CD a mi hermano
I gave my sister a scarf..Di a mi hermana una bufanda
What did you do on your birthday? ....¿Qué hiciste para celebrar tu cumpleaños?
I went out for a meal with my family..................Salí a comer con mi familia
What presents did you get?.................................¿Qué regalos recibiste?
My parents gave me … ....Mis padres me dieron …

Weather - short answers

What is the weather like?	¿Qué tiempo hace?
It is fine	Hace buen tiempo
It is hot	Hace calor
It is cold	Hace frío
The weather is bad	Hace mal tiempo
It is 30 degrees	Hace treinta grados
It is sunny	Hace sol
It is windy	Hace viento
It is foggy	Hay niebla
It is freezing	Hay helada
It is stormy	Hay tormentas
It is cloudy	Está nublado
It is snowing	Está nevando
It is raining	Está lloviendo

What was the weather like?	¿Qué tiempo hacía?
It was fine	Hacía buen tiempo
It was hot	Hacía calor
It was cold	Hacía frío
The weather was bad	Hacía mal tiempo
It was sunny	Hacía sol
It was windy	Hacía viento
It was foggy	Había niebla
It was freezing	Había helada
It was stormy	Había tormentas
It was cloudy	Estaba nublado
It was snowing	Estaba nevando
It was raining	Estaba lloviendo
It reached 30 degrees	Alcanzó los treinta grados

What will the weather be like?	**¿Qué tiempo hará?**
It will be fine	Hará buen tiempo
It will be hot	Hará calor
It will be cold	Hará frío
The weather will be bad	Hará mal tiempo
It will be sunny	Hará sol
It will be windy	Hará viento
It will be foggy	Habrá niebla
It will freeze	Habrá helada
It will be stormy	Habrá tormentas
It will be cloudy	Estará nublado
It will snow	Estará nevando
It will rain	Estará lloviendo
It will reach 30 degrees	Alcanzará los treinta grados

Weather - longer answers

¿Qué estación del año prefieres?
What season do you like best?

Prefiero el verano porque me gusta el sol. Me gusta dar paseos. Me gusta ir a orillas del mar. ¡No aguanto el frío del invierno! Odio la niebla y la lluvia.

Prefiero el invierno porque me chifla esquiar. Me gustan mucho la nieve y las montañas. En el verano no me gusta el calor.

Making comparisons between Spain and England

You may be asked to compare and contrast aspects of life in Spain and England. Here are some points you may find useful.

School life

School starts earlier in the morning in Spain	Las clases empiezan más temprano por la mañana en España
They do not finish until 5.00 pm	No terminan hasta las cinco
The school day is very long in Spain	El día escolar es muy largo en España
We have to wear school uniform	Tenemos que llevar uniforme
Spanish pupils get a lot of homework	Los alumnos españoles tienen muchos deberes
Spanish pupils sometimes repeat a year	A veces los alumnos españoles tienen que repetir de curso
The summer holidays are longer in Spain	Las vacaciones de verano son más largas en España
In the summer holidays many Spanish children take part in organised holidays	Durante las vacaciones de verano muchos niños españoles participan en vacaciones organizadas

Daily life

People eat later in the evening in Spain	Se cena más tarde en España
I prefer to eat earlier in the evening	Prefiero comer más temprano por la noche
I don't like sitting at table for a long time	No me gusta sentarme a la mesa mucho tiempo
The weather is warmer in Spain	Hace más calor en España
More people smoke in Spain	Hay más gente que fuma en España
I don't like the TV programmes	No me gustan los programas de televisión
Films start later in the evening in Spanish cinemas	Las películas empiezan más tarde en los cines españoles

Travel

Public transport is better in Spain	Los transportes públicos son mejores en España
You have to pay to go on the motorways in Spain	Hay que pagar para utilizar las autopistas en España
There are more lorries on the motorways in the UK	Hay más camiones en las autopistas en el Reino Unido

Your own presentation

SECTION 3: PRESENTATIONS

Suitable presentation-style answers could be prepared by using some of the themes in the conversation section, but you could also choose other topics if you have to do a presentation for your GCSE board's examination. Here are a few possibilities:

Mis prácticas laborales

Hace un mes hice una semana de prácticas laborales en una oficina en el centro de la ciudad.
Por la mañana me levanté a las siete, me duché y me vestí. Llevaba (*here you can describe what you wore*). Tomé (*say what you ate and drank*) para el desayuno.
Salí de casa a las ocho y cuarto. Fui a la oficina (*give form of transport*) y llegué a las nueve menos diez.
En la oficina preparé café para los otros empleados.
Luego me ocupé del correo con la secretaria del jefe.
Después tuve que archivar los documentos.
A las doce y media fui a la ciudad para comer con un amigo que hacía sus prácticas en un banco. (*say what you ate and drank*)
Par la tarde fui a Correos para comprar sellos para la secretaria.
No fue muy interesante como trabajo, pero todos los empleados fueron simpáticos.
Volví a casa a (*state time*).

El trimestre pasado pasé una semana de prácticas laborales en un garaje en mi aldea. El jefe es amigo di mi padre. Me gustaba mucho pasar una semana en un garaje porque me chiflan los coches y las motocicletas.
Por la mañana me levanté a (*state time*), tomé el desayuno (*say what you ate and drank*).
Me vestí (*say what you wore*) para ir al garaje, y salí de casa a (*say time*). Llegué a las ocho menos cinco. Fui al garaje (*give form of transport*). Primero preparé té para los mecánicos. Después observé a un mecánico que reparaba un coche. Fue interesante.
Hacia el fin de la semana limpié el coche del jefe. Es un coche magnífico. ¡Espero tener uno parecido un día de estos!

Mi cumpleaños

Mi cumpleaños es el veinticuatro de julio. Es a principios de las vacaciones de verano. Me gusta ir de excursión si hace buen tiempo. El año pasado era un sábado, así es que decidí ir a pasar el día en el campo con mi familia y unos amigos/unas amigas. Salimos a las nueve. Eramos diez personas. Mi padre y mi hermano conducían los dos coches. Mi madre y yo preparamos la merienda - jamón, huevos duros, tomates, ensalada, frambuesas y zumo de fruta y Tri-Naranjus® para beber. Hacía buen tiempo, el sol brillaba. Después de una hora llegamos a orillas del mar. Fuimos a la playa. Nadamos y jugamos al voleibol. A mediodía comimos. A eso de las dos dimos un paseo a lo largo de los acantilados. Nos paramos en una cafetería donde compramos helados. Volvimos muy tarde a casa. Fue un día muy agradable.

El fin de semana

Me gusta mucho el fin de semana porque tengo tiempo para hacer lo que me gusta. Durante la semana tengo muchos deberes, así es que no tengo tiempo para salir. Cuando tengo tiempo libre me gusta dar paseos con mis amigos/amigas. Vamos a la ciudad, pero también damos paseos en las colinas cuando hace buen tiempo. Si me quedo en casa, me gusta escuchar música *(Here you can talk about your favourite type of music)* o leo novelas. *(Here you must be prepared to talk briefly about a book or type of novel you like)*

Los sábados por la mañana trabajo en una escuela de baile. Hay mucha gente que viene para clases de ballet, de disco o de swing. *(You could describe one or two of them)*

Los sábados por la tarde voy con mis amigos/amigas a Worcester. Vamos a bailar. A veces me pongo una mini-falda roja y una blusa negra, a veces me pongo un pantalón marrón con una camiseta color naranja.

El sábado pasado fuimos a *(town name)*. Llevaba puesto *(Say what you wore)* Comimos patatas fritas, bebimos zumo de limón y fuimos a una sala de fiestas. Bailamos hasta medianoche.

La semana que viene iré con mis amigos a ver la película *(Put in the title)*. Es una película *(put in what type and say what it is about)* Vamos a salir por la tarde y llegaremos a *(town)* a las seis. La sesión empieza a las siete y media y la película dura dos horas. Después de la película cogeremos el autobús para volver a casa.

El tiempo libre

Me gusta hacer bricolaje cuando tengo tiempo libre. Siempre me gustaban las clases en las que trabajaba con madera o metal cuando estaba en séptimo u octavo de EGB. Se nos enseñaba a utilizar las herramientas para construir modelos u objetos para regalar. Construí un barco pequeño que di a mi hermano. En este momento estoy haciendo una colección de guerreros de fantasía de metal.

Los compro, los pego y finalmente los pinto. Es un trabajo muy largo. Me hace falta paciencia. A mi hermana no le gusta hacer bricolaje. Dice que es tiempo perdido.

Me gusta hacer deportes. Los sábados por la mañana me entreno con el club de *(Insert sport)*. Normalmente hay un partido los domingos por la tarde. Prefiero ganar, pero no ganamos muy a menudo, desafortunadamente.

Estoy aprendiendo a tocar el trombón desde hace tres años. Toco en la charanga del colegio. Tocamos mucha música moderna. Es fenomenal.

El fútbol

Me chifla jugar al fútbol. Juego en el equipo del colegio desde hace cuatro años. Me entreno cada sábado. Nuestro entrenador era jugador profesional, y nos ha enseñado mucho. Soy extremo derecho. El equipo del colegio jugó en la final del torneo de los colegios, pero desafortunadamente perdimos. Fuimos a jugar a Wembley. Fue un día maravilloso.

Soy hincha de *(Here you can put in the team of your choice!)* Es un equipo de primera división. Lleva *(Here you can put in the colours of your team's strip)*. Veo muchos partidos en la televisión porque tenemos antena parabólica.

Me gustaría ser jugador profesional. Si tienes éxito ganas mucho dinero y puedes ir a jugar en otros países del mundo.

La equitación

Me gusta mucho hacer equitación. Tengo una amiga que vive en una granja cerca de mi casa y tiene dos caballos. Durante el verano damos paseos a caballo todos los días a las cuatro cuando terminan las clases.
Los caballos se llaman Benji y Fleur. Benji tiene diez años, salta muy bien y ha ganado muchos premios. Fleur tiene veinte años y es bastante gorda porque come demasiada hierba en la primavera, pero es muy mansa.
Cuando se trata de los caballos hay que trabajar duro. Tenemos que darles de comer y limpiar el cuadro. La paja, el alimento y la silla no son ligeros, así es que se debe ser bastante fuerte para hacer este tipo de trabajo.
Durante la primavera Fleur sufría. Tosía y yo debía darle jarabe. No quería tragarlo. Me sentía desgraciado/a.
El año que viene quisiera comprar un caballo para mí. Sin duda no será un caballo de pura sangre. Cierto que será un caballo, no muy joven, pero lo importante es esté bien de salud y que tenga buenos cascos negros. Es muy importante porque cuesta mucho el veterinario o el herrero.

Mi intercambio escolar

Hace dos años hice un intercambio escolar. Fui a pasar dos semanas en casa de mi corresponsal que vive en una aldea pequeña cerca de Sevilla a orillas del río Guadalquivir. Es una región de viñas. Es una región donde hay inundaciones de vez en cuando en el invierno.
Mi corresponsal se llama ... *(Here you can give the name and age of your penfriend)*
Es *(Give a description of him/her)*
Tiene *(Here you can give details of his/her brothers and sisters)*
La casa es bastante grande. Hay cuatro dormitorios, un comedor, un salón, el cuarto de baño y la cocina. El jardín es muy grande y baja hasta la orilla del río. Hay muchas flores y árboles en el jardín.
La aldea donde viven es pequeña. Hay una iglesia grande, Correos, una panadería y un supermercado.
Durante mi visita, fui a Sevilla. Vi la catedral, la Torre de Oro y las tiendas. Hicimos una excursión a Granada. *(Add a few sentences here about a day at the seaside. Say what you ate and drank; say what the weather was like)*

El día de la boda de mi hermana

El mes de agosto fue muy interesante para mi familia el año pasado. Mi hermana se casó el día doce de agosto. Había decidido casarse en agosto porque es maestra. Su novio Robert es policía. Durante unos meses habló con mi madre de vestidos, regalos, flores y fotos.
El día de la boda hizo buen tiempo. El sol brilló e hizo calor.
La boda civil tuvo lugar a la una en el Ayuntamiento y a las dos y media fue la bendición en la iglesia. ¡Después de todo eso fue la hora de las fotos! Dura mucho tiempo, la sesión de fotos de una boda.
El vestido de mi hermana era muy bonito y llevaba unas flores hermosas. Las damas de honor llevaban vestidos azules. Me gustaba el vestido que llevaba. El azul es mi color preferido.
Después de las fotos fuimos al banquete de boda. Comí mucho - había salmón, pavo real y ensaladas de todo tipo. Por la tarde bailamos hasta las diez y media.

Proteger el medio ambiente

Debemos prestar atención. Hay demasiada polución en el mundo. Malgastamos los recursos naturales. El estilo de vida en Europa y en los Estados Unidos utiliza mucha energía. Algunas de nuestras industrias, de nuestras refinerías, de nuestras centrales nucleares envenenan el medio ambiente. Todo el mundo debe tratar de hacer todo lo posible para cambiar la situación. Por ejemplo: mi padre dice que cuando vamos a la ciudad debemos ir a pie o en bici en vez de sacar el coche y si vamos a Worcester deberíamos utilizar los transportes públicos más bien que el coche.

Mi madre nos dice que nos pongamos un jersey en vez de encender la calefacción cuando hace un poco frío.

Reciclamos las latas, las botellas y los periódicos.

También se pueden escoger productos ecológicos para lavar la ropa y fregar los platos.

For general reference for all topics:

Page 2	Expressing likes and dislikes
Page 45	Weather

If you wish to choose other subjects for your presentation, help with these topics can be found:

Page 28	Yourself and your family
Page 28	Describing a friend
Page 30	Your home
Page 31	Your home town and its surroundings
Page 34	Daily routine
Page 37	School and future plans
Page 40	Free time and hobbies
Page 41	Fitness and health
Page 43	Holidays

SECTION 4: IMPROVING YOUR LANGUAGE

When?

after ....después
afterwards, then ....luego, entonces
all day long ....todo el día
all morning ....toda la mañana
always ....siempre
at the end of ....al final de
at the weekend ....los fines de semana
during the morning/weekend ....durante la mañana/el fin de semana
at last ....por fin
before ....antes
early ....temprano
every day ....todos los días
every Monday morning ....todos los lunes por la mañana
every two days ....cada dos días
every week ....cada semana
every three weeks ....cada tres semanas
from time to time, occasionally ....de vez en cuando
in the morning ....por la mañana
late ....tarde
never ....nunca
now ....ahora
often ....a menudo
on Saturday mornings ....los sábados por la mañana
rarely, seldom ....rara vez
sometimes ....a veces
soon ....pronto
then ....entonces
this morning ....esta mañana
this summer/this winter ....este verano/este invierno
today ....hoy
usually ....normalmente

Phrases for telling stories in the past

a few weeks ago ....hace unas semanas
after finishing his/her homework … ....después de terminar sus deberes …
an hour ago ....hace una hora
a quarter of an hour ago ....hace un cuarto de hora
a short time later ....poco después
as he/she was leaving the house … ....al salir de casa …
as soon as possible ....cuanto antes

at five o'clock .... a las cinco
at that moment .... en ese momento
at the beginning of the holidays .... a principios de las vacaciones
at the end of the day .... al final del día
a week/month/two years ago .... hace una semana/un mes/dos años
during his stay in hospital .... durante su estancia en el hospital
during the summer holidays .... durante las vacaciones de verano
for a long time .... mucho tiempo
for three hours .... por tres horas
from time to time .... de vez en cuando
half an hour later .... media hora más tarde
immediately after the picnic … .... inmediatamente después de la merienda …
in spring/in summer .... en la primavera/en el verano
in autumn/in winter .... en el otoño/en el invierno
It was 1st December .... Fue el primero de diciembre
It was Christmas Eve. .... Era Nochebuena
It was during the Easter holidays .... Fue durante las vacaciones de Pascuas
yesterday .... ayer
the day before yesterday .... anteayer
yesterday morning/afternoon/evening .... ayer por la mañana/ayer por la tarde
last night .... anoche
last Saturday .... el sábado pasado
last week/last year .... la semana pasada/el año pasado
last winter .... el invierno pasado
later than usual .... más tarde que normal
some time later/after some time .... después de un rato
that morning/that afternoon/that evening .... aquella mañana/tarde/noche
the next day .... el día siguiente
towards the end of the week .... a finales de la semana
two days later .... dos días más tarde
towards the end of August .... a fines de agosto
On leaving the shop … .... Al salir de la tienda …
She left at once .... Se marcho inmediatamente
He had got up early because … .... Se había levantado temprano porque …
He appeared suddenly .... Se presentó de repente
I saw him just now .... Le vi hace un momento

Phrases for telling stories in the future

earlier/later than usual .... más temprano/tarde que lo normal
from time to time .... de vez en cuando
from this time on .... desde hoy en adelante
immediately/at once .... inmediatamente/enseguida
in half an hour's time .... en media hora

in an hour and a half .... en una hora y media
two hours from now .... en dos horas
later on today .... más tarde hoy
towards seven o'clock this evening .... hacia las siete esta tarde
tomorrow/the day after tomorrow .... mañana/pasado mañana
tomorrow morning .... mañana por la mañana
tomorrow afternoon/evening .... mañana por la tarde
in three days' time .... en tres días
next Sunday .... el domingo que viene
in a week's time .... en una semana
this time next week .... de hoy en ocho días
next week/next year .... la semana/el año que viene
next winter .... el invierno que viene
She will be arriving about midday .... Llegará a eso de mediodía
The train will be arriving on time .... El tren llegará puntualmente

How did you do that?

also .... también
at top speed .... a máxima velocidad
as soon as possible .... cuanto antes
by chance .... por casualidad
carefully .... con cuidado
for the first/last time .... por primera/última vez
for the second time .... por segunda vez
gladly .... con mucho gusto
gradually .... poco a poco
happily/fortunately .... afortunadamente
in a good/bad temper .... de buen/mal humor
in vain .... en vano
Instead of going to school … .... En vez de ir al insti(tuto) …
I pretended to read my book .... Fingí leer mi libro
I went in on tip-toe .... Entré de puntillas
quickly .... de prisa
politely .... con cortesía
slowly .... despacio
suddenly .... de repente
thus .... así
to my great surprise .... con gran sorpresa mía
unfortunately .... desafortunadamente
When everything was ready … .... Cuando todo estaba listo …
without hesitation .... sin vacilar
without speaking .... sin hablar
without saying a word .... sin decir nada

With astonishment, I ... . Con asombro, yo ...
without wasting any time .... sin perder tiempo

Where?

above .... encima de
against/on the wall .... contra/en el muro
at the seaside .... a orillas del mar
behind the house .... detrás de la casa
under the bridge .... debajo del puente
between the trees .... entre los árboles
here .... aquí
in front of the cinema .... delante del cine
in the country .... en el campo
in the distance .... en la distancia
in the middle of the town .... en el centro del pueblo/de la ciudad
in the mountains .... en las montañas
in the meadow .... en el prado
in the woods .... en el bosque
nearby .... cerca
near my home .... cerca de mi casa
near the lift .... cerca del ascensor
next to the bank .... al lado del banco
on the balcony .... en el balcón
on the first floor .... en el primer piso
on the ground floor .... en la planta baja
on the horizon .... en el horizonte
on the river bank .... en la orilla del río
on the top floor .... en el último piso
opposite the station .... enfrente de la estación
over there .... allá
100 metres away .... a cien metros
ten minutes away .... a diez minutos
there .... allí
this/that way .... por aquí/por allí
to/in the north .... al/en el norte
to/in the south .... al/en el sur
to/in the east .... al/en el este
to/in the west .... al/en el oeste
to the left of the house.. .... a la izquierda de la casa
to the right of the window .... a la derecha de la ventana

Who was there?

an old man .... un viejo
a young woman .... una mujer joven
a little boy who was about seven .... un niño de unos siete años
an elderly woman with grey hair .... una vieja con el pelo gris
a tall girl who was wearing a red coat .... una chica alta que llevaba un abrigo rojo
a short fat man with a black beard .... un hombre bajo y gordo con barba negra
a girl of about sixteen who was carrying a big bag .... una chica de unos dieciséis años que llevaba un bolso grande
a middle-aged woman/aged about fifty who was walking her dog .... una mujer de mediana edad/de unos cincuenta años que paseaba su perro
a man wearing sunglasses driving a blue Renault .... un hombre con gafas de sol que conducía un Renault azul
two teenage girls talking to someone who seemed worried .... dos chicas adolescentes que hablaban con alguien que parecía preocupado

What did he/she look like?

He had a moustache .... Tenía bigote
He had a long black beard .... Tenía una barba larga y negra
He had black/fair/brown/grey/ginger hair .... Tenía el pelo negro/rubio/moreno/gris/rojo
He was tall/small/thin/fat .... Era alto/pequeño/delgado/gordo
He was wearing a blue suit .... Llevaba un traje azul
He was carrying a black umbrella .... Llevaba un paraguas negro
He was frowning .... Fruncía el ceño

She was tall/small/thin/fat/slim .... Era alta/pequeña/delgada/gorda/esbelta
She looked happy/stressed/frightened .... Parecía contenta/estresada/asustada
She had blue/green/grey/brown eyes .... Tenía los ojos azules/verdes/grises/marrones
She was wearing glasses/sunglasses .... Llevaba gafas/gafas de sol
She was wearing jeans and a red T-shirt .... Llevaba vaqueros y una camiseta roja
She was smiling .... Sonreía
She was crying .... Lloraba

What did I have to eat and drink?

I drank a cup of coffee .... Bebí una taza de café
I had a glass of lemonade .... Tomé un vaso de limonada
I had a chocolate ice cream .... Tomé un helado de chocolate
I bought a ham sandwich .... Compré un bocadillo de jamón
I bought some cheese, tomatoes, apples and a packet of crisps .... Compré queso, tomates, manzanas y un paquete de patatas fritas
I ordered roast chicken .... Pedí pollo asado
He chose an omelette sandwich .... Escogió un bocadillo de tortilla
She preferred steak and chips .... Prefería un biftec con patatas fritas

We went to a restaurant because it was my birthday .... Fuimos a un restaurante porque era mi cumpleaños
We decided to have a picnic .... Decidimos hacer un picnic
We ordered two Tri-Naranjus® .... Pedimos dos Tri-Naranjus®

Sequences

at first .... al principio
secondly .... en segundo lugar
thirdly .... en tercer lugar
then .... luego
after that .... después de eso
after doing that .... después de hacer eso
He had just done that when … .... Acababa de hacer eso cuando …
a little later .... poco después
after a while .... después de un rato
a few minutes later .... unos minutos después
later that day .... más tarde aquel día
later that evening .... más tarde aquella tarde
two hours later .... dos horas más tarde
After arriving in Dover … .... Después de llegar en Dover …
on the first part of the journey .... en la primera parte del viaje
on the last part of the journey .... en la última parte del viaje
on the first/last day of the holiday .... el primer/último día de las vacaciones
at half past one .... a la una y media
as arranged .... como había sido planeado
during the morning/afternoon/evening .... durante la mañana/tarde/noche
during the night .... durante la noche
the next day .... el día siguiente
the next morning .... la mañana siguiente
the day after tomorrow .... pasado mañana

Conclusions

at the end of the day .... al final del día
at the end of the outing .... al final de la excursión
at the end of the show .... al final del espectáculo
at last/finally .... por fin
in spite of everything .... a pesar de todo
We arrived home tired but happy .... Llegamos a casa cansados pero contentos
We arrived home tired but happy .... Llegamos a casa cansadas pero contentas
We had had a good time .... Lo habíamos pasado bomba

Notes

Notes